S. Hrg. 113–479

THE AUTHORIZATION OF USE OF FORCE IN SYRIA

HEARING

BEFORE THE

COMMITTEE ON FOREIGN RELATIONS UNITED STATES SENATE

ONE HUNDRED THIRTEENTH CONGRESS

FIRST SESSION

SEPTEMBER 3, 2013

Printed for the use of the Committee on Foreign Relations

Available via the World Wide Web:
http://www.fdsys.gpo.gov

U.S. GOVERNMENT PRINTING OFFICE

91–222 PDF   WASHINGTON : 2014

For sale by the Superintendent of Documents, U.S. Government Printing Office
Internet: bookstore.gpo.gov   Phone: toll free (866) 512–1800; DC area (202) 512–1800
Fax: (202) 512–2104   Mail: Stop IDCC, Washington, DC 20402–0001

(II)

CONTENTS

THE AUTHORIZATION OF USE
OF FORCE IN SYRIA

TUESDAY, SEPTEMBER 3, 2013

U.S. SENATE,
COMMITTEE ON FOREIGN RELATIONS,
Washington, DC

The committee met, pursuant to notice, at 2:38 p.m., in Room SH-216, Hart Senate Office Building, Hon. Robert Menendez, chairman of the committee, presiding.

PRESENT. Senators Menendez [presiding], Boxer, Cardin, Shaheen, Coons, Durbin, Udall, Murphy, Kaine, Markey, Corker, Risch, Rubio, Johnson, Flake, McCain, Barrasso, and Paul.

OPENING STATEMENT OF HON. ROBERT MENENDEZ, U.S. SENATOR FROM NEW JERSEY

The CHAIRMAN. This hearing of the Senate Foreign Relations Committee will come to order.

Let me first say that—neither actions of approval or disapproval from the audience. We welcome you to be here on this important occasion, but we welcome you to be observers of this important occasion. And the chair will not tolerate actions that are in violation of the committee rules.

Let me welcome Secretary Kerry back to the committee that he chaired, Secretary Hagel on a committee that he served on, and the Chairman of the Joint Chiefs of Staff, General Dempsey, to the committee.

We convene this hearing, as we have convened many before, to make one of the most difficult decisions we are asked and tasked to make—the authorization of the use of American military power. This time in Syria to respond to the horrific chemical attack of August 21st that took the lives of 1,429 Syrians, including at least 426 children.

The images of that day are sickening, and in my view, the world cannot ignore the inhumanity and the horror of this act. I do not take our responsibility to authorize military force lightly or make such decisions easily. I voted against the war in Iraq and strongly have supported a withdrawal of U.S. troops from Afghanistan. But today, I support the President's decision to use military force in the face of this horrific crime against humanity.

Yes, there are risks to action, but the consequences of inaction are greater and graver still: Further humanitarian disaster in Syria, regional instability, the loss of American credibility around the world, an emboldened Iran and North Korea, and a disintegration of international law.

This decision will be one of the most difficult any of us will be asked to make, but it is our role as representatives of the American people to make it, to put aside political differences and personal ideologies, to forget partisanship and preconceptions, to forget the polls, the politics, and even personal consequences. It is a moment for a profile in courage and to do what one knows is right.

It is our responsibility to evaluate the facts, assess the intelligence we have, and then debate the wisdom and scope of a military response fully and publicly, understanding its geopolitical ramifications and fully aware of the consequences. At the end of the day, each of us will decide whether to vote for or against a resolution for military action based on our assessments of the facts and our conscience.

The decision rests with us. It is not political. It is a policy decision that must be based, I believe, on what we believe is in the national security interests of the United States.

To be clear, the authorization we will ultimately seek is for focused action with a clear understanding that American troops will not be on the ground in combat, and the language before us is but a starting point.

The President has decided to ask Congress for our support. Now the eyes of the world are upon us. The decision we make, the resolution we present to the Senate, and the votes we take will reverberate around the world.

Our friends and allies await our decision, as does the despot in Pyongyang, the ayatollahs of terror in Tehran, and terrorist groups wherever they may be. What we do in the face of the chemical attack by the Assad regime against innocent civilians will send a signal to the world that such weapons in violation of international law cannot be used with impunity.

The question is, will we send a message that the United States will not tolerate the use of chemical weapons anywhere in the world, by anyone, for any reason? Will we, in the name of all that is human and decent, authorize the use of American military power against the inexcusable, indiscriminate, and immoral use of chemical weapons? Or will we stand down?

What message do we send the world when such a crime goes unpunished? Will those who have these weapons use them again? Will they use them more widely and kill more children? Will they use them against our allies, against our troops or embassies? Or will they give them or sell them to terrorists who would use them against us here at home?

Are we willing to watch a slaughter just because the patrons of that slaughter are willing to use their veto at the United Nations to allow it to happen so their beneficiary can stay in power? And are we so tired of war that we are willing to silence our conscience and accept the consequences that will inevitably flow from that silence to our national interests?

We will hear the arguments and the options presented to us today, and we will look at the facts as we know them according to the declassified assessment released last Friday that Secretary Kerry has so passionately presented to the Nation. According to that assessment, we know with high confidence from the intelligence community that the Syrian government carried out a chemical weapons attack in the Damascus suburbs on August 21st.

We know that the Assad regime has stockpiled chemical agents, including mustard, sarin, and VX gas, and has thousands of munitions capable of delivering them. We know that President Bashar al-Assad makes the decisions when it comes to the regime's stockpile of chemical agents and that personnel involved in the program are carefully vetted to ensure loyalty to the regime and the security of the program.

We have evidence that chemical weapons have been used on a smaller scale against the opposition on several other occasions in the past year, including in the Damascus suburbs, that sarin gas has been used on some of those occasions and that it was not the opposition that used it.

We know that chemical weapons personnel from the Syrian Scientific Studies and Research Center, subordinate to the regime's Ministry of Defense, were operating in the Damascus suburb of Adra from Sunday, August 18th until early in the morning on Wednesday, August 21st near an area the regime uses to mix chemical weapons, including sarin.

And human intelligence as well as signal and geospatial intelligence have shown regime activity in the preparation of chemicals prior to the attack, including the distribution and use of gas masks.

We have multiple streams of intelligence that show the regime launched a rocket attack against the Damascus suburbs in the early hours of August 21st, and satellite corroboration that the attacks were launched from a regime-controlled area and struck neighborhoods where the chemical attacks reportedly occurred, clearly tying the pieces together. That is what we know in terms of who deployed these weapons.

More evidence is available, and we will be looking at all of the classified information in a closed session of the committee tomorrow that more clearly establishes the use of chemical weapons by the regime, the military responses available to us, and the results we expect from those responses.

But as of now, in my view, there is a preponderance of evidence beyond a reasonable doubt that Assad's forces willfully targeted civilians with chemical weapons. Having said that, at the end of the day, the chemical weapons attack against innocent civilians in Syria is an indirect attack on America's security, with broader implications for the region and the world.

If chemical weapons can be used with impunity in violation of a Geneva protocol crafted by the League of Nations and signed by the United States in 1925—in fact, signed by Syria itself in 1968—they can be used without fear of reprisal anywhere, by anyone. And in my view, such heinous and immoral violations of decency demand a clear and unambiguous response.

We are at a crossroads moment. A precedent will be set either for the unfettered and unpunished use of chemical weapons, or a precedent will be set for the deterrence of the use of such weapons through the limited use of military force that sends a message that the world will not stand down.

We will either send a message to Syria, Iran, North Korea, Hezbollah, al-Qaeda, and any other nonstate actors that the world will not tolerate the senseless use of chemical weapons by anyone, or we will choose to stand silent in the face of horrific human suffering.

We need to consider the consequences of not acting. Our silence would be a message to the Ayatollah that America and the world are not serious about stopping their march to acquiring nuclear weapons. Israel would no longer believe that we have their back and would be hard pressed to restrain itself.

Our silence would embolden Kim Jong-un, who has a large chemical weapons cache, and would send a message that we are not serious about protecting South Korea and the region from nuclear or chemical weapons, and would embolden Hezbollah and Hamas to redouble their efforts to acquire chemical weapons, and they might succeed.

Clearly, at the end of the day, our national security is at stake.

I want to thank our distinguished witnesses who will present the facts as they know them. We will evaluate them, debate a resolution, and at the end of the day, each of us will decide whether to send a message to the world that there are lines we cannot cross as civilized human beings or stand silent and risk new threats.

Let me say before I turn to Senator Corker for his opening statement, the President is asking for an authorization for the use of limited force. It is not his intention or ours to involve ourselves fully in Syria's civil war.

What is before us is a request, and I quote, ''to prevent or deter the use or proliferation of chemical or biological weapons within, to, or from Syria and to protect the United States and its allies and partners against the threat posed by such weapons.''

This is not a declaration of war, but a declaration of our values to the world. A declaration that says we are willing to use our military power when necessary against anyone who dares turn such heinous weapons on innocent civilians anywhere in the world.

We know the facts. We will hear the arguments. We will have the debate, and then it will be up to each of us to search our conscience and make a decision on behalf of the American people. I trust that we can achieve that in a bipartisan way.

I have been working with Senator Corker as we move toward a resolution, but I hope we will get broad bipartisan support. And before I turn to him, I just want to acknowledge the presence, and we are thrilled to see her here today, of Teresa Heinz Kerry to join us in this momentous occasion. I am glad to see you so well and being here with us.

And with that, Senator Corker.

OPENING STATEMENT OF HON. BOB CORKER, U.S. SENATOR FROM TENNESSEE

Senator CORKER. Mr. Chairman, I thank you for your comments and the time that we spent together recently.

And I want to thank our witnesses for being here not only for their service to our country in their current capacity, but in their service in every way for many, many years. I thank you for being here.

Today, you are beginning the formal request of asking each of us to make the most important decision many of us will make during our tenure in the United States Senate. And I know that everybody here on the dais and those who are not take that decision very seriously.

I have noticed a distinct sense of humility as we have gone about the various questions, conference calls, the earlier meetings we have had today and previously this week, and I know that every member here knows that whether they decide to support an authorization for the use of military force or not, they are making a decision about our country's national interests. And I know that everybody is going to be taking that decision very, very seriously.

One of the issues that many members will have is the fact that should we support an authorization for the use of military force— and I think that everyone here knows that I am very generally inclined to do so and am working closely with Senator Menendez for something that will be a starting point for this committee's discussions, and I know each member will have input and will have the opportunity to put thier imprint on what it is that we end up deciding to vote upon—but one of the problems that members have, and I think this hearing and tomorrow's hearing is important to answer, is while we make policy, you implement policy. And the implementation of this is very, very important, and I think there have been mixed signals about what that implementation actually is going to mean and the effect it is going to have on the country that we are involved in.

I want to say that I was just in the region, as I know many people have been, and I am still totally dismayed by the lack of support we are giving to the vetted moderate opposition. We publicly stated what that support is going to be, even though it is being carried out in a covert way.

But it is to some degree humiliating to be in a refugee camp when our policy has been that we are going to train, we are going to equip, we are going to give humanitarian aid to the vetted opposition, and yet when you sit down with the people who are coalescing around this, like General Idris and others, very little of that has occurred.

So I know today's focus is going to be largely on the issue of chemical warfare, and I know that the case has to be made, and I know that each of us has had the opportunity to hear that case, to see the intelligence, to understand on what basis these claims have been made. And my guess is that most everyone here fully believes that chemical weapons have been used on civilians to a large degree.

So I know that case is going to be made to the American people today, as you are making it to us. But it is my hope that a big part of what you are going to do here today, and I know we talked about this earlier this morning at the White House, but is to make a case as to why Syria is important to our national interests, why Syria matters to the region, why it is important for us to carry out this stated strategy, and how we are going to continue to carry out that stated strategy.

One of the things that I do not want to see in this authorization is after - if it is authorized and force takes place-I want to see us, I want to see us continue to carry out the strategy that has been stated, and that is building the capacity of the vetted moderate opposition. So I would like to have you address that.

I would like to have you today also address how this use of military force supports that strategy, how it is going to affect the region in the aftermath.

So I thank you for being here today. I know a big part of what we are discussing today is the effect that our decisions will have on the credibility of the United States of America. I know that people in the region are watching. I know that we have been hesitant to move on with many of the activities that we have stated we are going to be carrying out.

So, today, I hope that each of you will bring clarity to this. I know we are going to talk about chemical warfare, but I hope you will give us even more clarity about our opposition strengthening, about how this is going to affect us overall, and I hope we will all leave here today with a clear understanding of how this strategy is going to be carried out.

I thank you, and I look forward to your testimony.

The CHAIRMAN. Secretary Kerry.

STATEMENT OF HON. JOHN F. KERRY, SECRETARY OF STATE, U.S. DEPARTMENT OF STATE, WASHINGTON, DC

Secretary KERRY. Well, Mr. Chairman, members of the committee, Ranking Member Corker, thank you very, very much for having us here today. We look forward to this opportunity to be able to share with you President Obama's vision with respect to not just this action but, as Senator Corker has inquired appropriately, about Syria itself and the course of action in the Middle East.

Mr. Chairman, thank you for welcoming Teresa. This is her first public event since early July. So we are all happy she is here.

As we convene for this debate, it is not an exaggeration to say to you—all of you, my former colleagues—that the world is watching not just to see what we decide, but it is watching to see how we make this decision, whether in a dangerous world we can still make our Government speak with one voice. They want to know if America will rise to this moment and make a difference.

And the question of whether to authorize our Nation to take military action is, as you have said, Mr. Chairman, and you have echoed, Mr. Ranking Member, this is obviously one of the most important decisions, one of the most important responsibilities of this committee or of any Senator in the course of a career.

The President and the administration appreciate that you have returned quickly to the Nation's capital to address it and that you are appropriately beginning a process of focusing with great care and great precision, which is the only way to approach the potential use of military power.

Ranking Member Corker, I know that you want to discuss, as you said, why Syria matters to our national security and our strategic interests beyond the compelling humanitarian reasons, and I look forward, with Secretary Hagel and General Dempsey, to laying that out here this afternoon.

But first, it is important to explain to the American people why we are here. It is important for people who may not have caught every component of the news over the course of the Labor Day weekend to join us, all of us, in focusing in on what is at stake here. That is why the President of the United States made the decision as he did, contrary to what many people thought he would do, of asking the Congress to join in this decision. We are stronger as a Nation when we do that.

So we are here because against multiple warnings from the President of the United States, from the Congress, from our friends and allies around the world, and even from Russia and Iran, the Assad regime, and only undeniably the Assad regime, unleashed an outrageous chemical attack against its own citizens. We are here because a dictator and his family's personal enterprise, in their lust to hold onto power, were willing to infect the air of Damascus with a poison that killed innocent mothers, and fathers, and hundreds of their children, their lives all snuffed out by gas in the early morning of August 21st.

Now, some people here and there amazingly have questioned the evidence of this assault on conscience. I repeat here again today that only the most willful desire to avoid reality can assert that this did not occur as described, or that the regime did not do it. It did happen, and the Assad regime did it.

Now, I remember Iraq. Secretary Hagel remembers Iraq. General Dempsey especially remembers Iraq. But Secretary Hagel and I and many of you sitting on the dais remember Iraq in a special way because we were here for that vote. We voted. And so we are especially sensitive, Chuck and I, to never again asking any member to take a vote on faulty intelligence.

And that is why our intelligence community has scrubbed and re-scrubbed the evidence. We have declassified unprecedented amounts of information, and we ask the American people and the rest of the world to judge that information. We can tell you beyond any reasonable doubt that our evidence proves the Assad regime prepared for this attack, issued instructions to prepare for this attack and warned its own forces to use gas masks. And we have physical evidence of where the rockets came from and when. Not one rocket landed in regime-controlled territory, not one. All of them landed in opposition-controlled or contested territory.

We have a map, physical evidence, showing every geographical point of impact, and that is concrete. Within minutes of the attack—90 I think to be precise, maybe slightly shorter—the social media exploded with horrific images of the damage that had been caused, men and women, the elderly, and children sprawled on a hospital floor with no wounds, no blood, but all dead. Those scenes of human chaos and desperation were not contrived. They were real. No one could contrive such a scene.

We are certain that none of the opposition has the weapons or capacity to affect a strike of this scale, particularly from the heart of regime territory. Just think about it in logical terms, common sense. With high confidence, our intelligence community tells us that after the strike, the regime issued orders to stop, and then fretted openly, we know, about the possibility of U.N. inspectors discovering evidence.

So then, they began to systematically try to destroy it, contrary to my discussion with their foreign minister, who said we have nothing to hide. I said, if you have nothing to hide, then let the inspectors in today and let it be unrestricted. It was not. They did not. It took four days of shelling before they finally allowed them in under a constrained pre-arranged structure. And we now have learned that the hair and blood samples from first responders in East Damascus has tested positive for signatures of sarin.

So, my colleagues, we know what happened. For all the lawyers, for all the former prosecutors, for all those who have sat on a jury, I can tell you that we know these things beyond the reasonable doubt that is the standard by which we send people to jail for the rest of their lives.

So we are here because of what happened two weeks ago, but we are also here because of what happened nearly a century ago in the darkest moments of World War I and after the horror of gas warfare when the vast majority of the world came together to declare in no uncertain terms that chemical weapons crossed the line of conscience, and they must be banned from use forever. Over the years that followed, over 180 countries, including Iran, Iraq, and Russia, agreed, and they joined the Chemical Weapons Convention. Even countries with whom we agree on little agreed on that conviction.

Now, some have tried to suggest that the debate we are having today is about President Obama's red line. I could not more forcefully state that is just plain and simply wrong. This debate is about the world's red line. It is about humanity's red line. And it is a red line that anyone with a conscience ought to draw.

This debate is also about Congress' own red line. You, the United States Congress, agreed to the Chemical Weapons Convention. You, the United States Congress, passed the Syria Accountability Act, which says Syria's chemical weapons ''threaten the security of the Middle East and the national security interests of the United States.'' You, the Congress, have spoken out about grave consequences if Assad, in particular, used chemical weapons. So I say to you, Senator Corker, that is one of the reasons why Syria is important.

And as we debate and the world watches, as you decide and the world wonders, not whether Assad's regime executed the worst chemical weapons attack of the 21st century. That fact, I think, is now beyond question. The world wonders whether the United States of America will consent through silence to standing aside while this kind of brutality is allowed to happen without consequence.

In the nearly 100 years since the first global commitment against chemical weapons, only two tyrants dared to cross the world's brightest line. Now Bashar al-Assad has become the third. And I think all of you know that history holds nothing but infamy for those criminals, and history reserves also very little sympathy for their enablers. So the reality is the gravity of this moment. That is the importance of the decision that this Congress faces and that the world is waiting to learn about in these next days.

Now, Ranking Member Corker asked a central question: Why should Americans care beyond what I have just said, which ought to be enough in the judgment of the President and this administration. Well, it is clear that in addition to what I have just mentioned about the Syria Accountability Act and the threat to the Middle

East, we cannot overlook the impact of chemical weapons and the danger that they pose to a particularly volatile area of the world in which we have been deeply invested for years because we have great friends there. We have allies there. We have deep interests there.

Since President Obama's policy is that Assad must go, it is not insignificant that to deprive Assad of the capacity to use chemical weapons, or to degrade the capacity to use those chemical weapons, actually deprives him of a lethal weapon in this ongoing civil war, and that has an impact. That can help to stabilize the region ultimately.

In addition, we have other important strategic national security interests, not just in the prevention of the proliferation of chemical weapons, but to avoid the creation of a safe haven in Syria or a base of operations for extremists to use these weapons against our friends. All of us know that the extremes of both sides are there waiting in the wings, working and pushing and fighting. They would be desperate to get their hands on these materials. And the fact is that if nothing happens to begin to change the equation or the current calculation, that area can become even more so an area of ungoverned space where those extremists threaten even the United States and, more immediately, if they get their hands on their weapons, allies and friends of ours, like Jordan, or Israel, or Lebanon, or others.

Forcing Assad to change his calculation about his ability to act with impunity can contribute to his realization that he cannot gas or shoot his way out of his predicament. And as I think you know, it has been the President's primary goal to achieve a negotiated resolution, but you got to have parties prepared to negotiate to achieve that.

Syria is also important because, quite simply, and I cannot put this to you more plainly than to just ask each of you to ask yourselves, if you are Assad or if you are any one of the other despots in that region, and the United States steps back from this moment together with our other allies and friends, what is the message? The message is that he has been granted impunity, the freedom to choose to use the weapons again or force us to go through this cycle again with who knows what outcome after once refusing it. We would have granted him the capacity to use these weapons against more people with greater levels of damage because we would have stood and stepped away.

As confidently as we know what happened in Damascus, my friends, on August 21st, we know that Assad would read our stepping away or our silence as an invitation to use those weapons with impunity. And in creating impunity, we will be creating opportunity, the opportunity for other dictators and/or terrorists to pursue their own weapon of mass destruction, including nuclear weapons.

I will tell you there are some people hoping that the United States Congress does not vote for this very limited request the President has put before you. Iran is hoping you look the other way. Our inaction would surely give them a permission slip for them to at least misinterpret our intention, if not to put it to the test. Hezbollah is hoping that isolationism will prevail. North

Korea is hoping that ambivalence carries the day. They are all listening for our silence.

And if we do not answer Assad today, we will erode a standard that has existed for those 100 years. In fact, we will erode a standard that has protected our own troops in war, and we will invite even more dangerous tests down the road.

Our allies and our partners are also counting on us in this situation—the people of Israel, of Jordan, of Turkey. Each look next door and they see that they are one stiff breeze away from the potential of being hurt, of their civilians being killed as a consequence of choices Assad might make in the absence of action. They anxiously await our assurance that our word means something. They await the assurance that if the children lined up in un-bloodied burial shrouds for their own children, that we would keep the world's promise. That is what they are hoping.

So the authorization that President Obama seeks is definitely in our national security interests. We need to send to Syria and to the world, to dictators and terrorists, to allies, and to civilians alike the unmistakable message that when the United States of America and the world say ''never again,'' we do not mean sometimes, we do not mean somewhere. Never means never.

So this is a vote for accountability. Norms and laws that keep the civilized world civil mean nothing if they are not enforced. As Justice Jackson said in his opening statement at the Nuremberg trials, ''The ultimate step in avoiding periodic wars, which are inevitable in a system of international lawlessness, is to make statesmen responsible to the law.'' If the world's worst despots see that they can flout with impunity prohibitions against the world's worst weapons, then those prohibitions are just pieces of paper. That is what we mean by accountability, and that is what we mean by we cannot be silent.

So let me be clear. President Obama is not asking America to go to war. And I say that sitting next to two men, Secretary Hagel and Chairman Dempsey, who know what war is. Senator McCain knows what war is. They know the difference between going to war and what President Obama is requesting now. We all agree there will be no American boots on the ground. The President has made crystal clear we have no intention of assuming responsibility for Syria's civil war. He is asking only for the power to make clear, to make certain, that the United States means what we say, that the world, when we join together in a multilateral statement, mean what we say. He is asking for authorization to degrade and deter Bashar al-Assad's capacity to use chemical weapons.

Now, some will undoubtedly ask, and I think appropriately, what about the unintended consequences of action? Some fear a retaliation that leads to a larger conflict. Well, let me put it bluntly. If Assad is arrogant enough, and I would say foolish enough, to retaliate to the consequences of his own criminal activity, the United States and our allies have ample ways to make him regret that decision without going to war. Even Assad's supporters, Russia and Iran, say publicly that the use of chemical weapons is unacceptable.

Now, some will also question the extent of our responsibility. To them I say, when someone kills and injures hundreds of children with a weapon the world has banned, we are all responsible. That is true because of treaties like the Geneva Convention and the Chemical Weapons Convention, and, for us, the Syria Accountability Act. But it is also true because we share a common humanity and a common decency.

This is not the time for arm chair isolationism. This is not the time to be spectators to slaughter. Neither our country nor our conscience can afford the cost of silence. We have spoken up against unspeakable horror many times in the past. Now we must stand up and act, and we must protect our security, protect our values, and lead the world with conviction that is clear about our responsibility.

Thank you.

The CHAIRMAN. Thank you, Mr. Secretary.

VOICE. The American people, they do not want—

The CHAIRMAN. The committee will be in order. The committee will be in order.

VOICE. We do not want to go to war. We do not want another war.

The CHAIRMAN. I would ask the police to restore order.

VOICE. Wait a minute. Nobody wants this war. Cruise missiles, launching cruise missiles is another war. The American people do not want this.

The CHAIRMAN. Secretary Hagel?

Secretary KERRY. Can I just before—you know, the first time I testified before this committee when I was 27 years old, I had feelings very similar to that protestor. And I would just say that is exactly why it is so important that we are all here having this debate, talking about these things before the country. And that the Congress itself will act representing the American people. And I think we all can respect those who have a different point of view, and we do.

The CHAIRMAN. Secretary Hagel?

STATEMENT OF HON. CHUCK HAGEL, SECRETARY OF DEFENSE, U.S. DEPARTMENT OF DEFENSE, WASHINGTON, DC

Secretary HAGEL. Mr. Chairman, thank you. Chairman Menendez, and Ranking Member Corker, members of the committee, as we all know, in the coming days Congress will debate how to respond to the most recent chemical weapons attack in Syria. A large-scale sarin gas assault perpetrated by the Syrian government against its own people.

As a former Senator and member of this committee, I welcome this debate, and I strongly support President Obama's decision to seek congressional authorization for the use of force in Syria.

As each of us knows, committing the country to using military force is the most difficult decision America's leaders can make, as Ranking Member Corker noted. All of those who are privileged to serve our Nation have a responsibility to ask tough questions before that commitment is made. The American people must be assured that their leaders are acting according to U.S. national interests, with well-defined military objectives, with an understanding of the risks and the consequences involved.

The President, along with his national security team, asked those tough questions before we concluded that the United States should take military action against Syria because of what the Assad regime has done.

I want to address how we reached this decision by clarifying the U.S. interests at stake, our military objectives, and the risks of not acting at this critical juncture.

As President Obama said, the use of chemical weapons in Syria is not only an assault on humanity; it is a serious threat to America's national security interests and those of our closest allies. The Syrian regime's use of chemical weapons poses grave risks to our friends and partners along Syria's borders, including Israel, Jordan, Turkey, Lebanon, and Iraq. If Assad is prepared to use chemical weapons against his own people, we have to be concerned that terrorist groups like Hezbollah, which has forces in Syria supporting the Assad regime, would acquire them and would use them.

That risk of chemical weapons proliferation poses a direct threat to our friends, our partners, and to U.S. personnel in the region. We cannot afford for Hezbollah or any terrorist group determined to strike the United States to have incentives to acquire or use chemical weapons.

The Syrian regime's actions risk eroding the nearly century-old international norm against the use of chemical weapons, which Secretary Kerry has noted, a norm that has helped protect the United States' homeland and American forces operating across the globe from those terrible weapons. Weakening this norm could embolden other regimes to acquire or use chemical weapons. For example, North Korea maintains a massive stockpile of chemical weapons that threatens our treaty ally, the Republic of Korea, and the 28,000 U.S. troops stationed there.

I have just returned from Asia where I had a very serious and long conversation with South Korea's defense minister about the threat, the real threat that North Korea's stockpile of chemical weapons presents to them. Our allies throughout the world must be assured that the United States will fulfill its security commitments.

Given these threats to our national security, the United States must demonstrate through our actions that the use of chemical weapons is unacceptable. The President has made clear that our military objectives in Syria would be to hold the Assad regime accountable, degrade its ability to carry out these kinds of attacks, and deter the regime from further use of chemical weapons.

The Department of Defense has developed military options to achieve these objectives, and we have positioned U.S. assets throughout the region to successfully execute this mission. We believe we can achieve them with a military action that would be limited in duration and scope. General Dempsey and I have assured the President that U.S. forces will be ready to act whenever the President gives the order.

We are also working with our allies and our partners in this effort, key partners, including France, Turkey, Saudi Arabia, United Arab Emirates, and friends in the region have assured us of their strong support of U.S. action.

In defining our military objectives, we have made clear that we are not seeking to resolve the underlying conflict in Syria through direct military force. Instead, we are contemplating actions that are tailored to respond to the use of chemical weapons. A political solution created by the Syrian people is the only way to ultimately end the violence in Syria. And Secretary Kerry is leading international efforts to help the parties in Syria move toward a negotiated transition, a transition that means a free and inclusive Syria.

We are also committed to doing more to assist the Syrian opposition, but Assad must be held accountable for using these weapons in defiance of the international community.

Having defined America's interests and our military objectives, we also must examine the risks and the consequences of action, as well as the consequences of inaction. There are always risks in taking action. The Assad regime, under increasing pressure by the Syrian opposition, could feel empowered to carry out even more devastating chemical weapons attacks without a response. Chemical weapons make no distinction between combatants and innocent civilians, and inflict the worst kind of indiscriminate suffering, as we have recently seen.

A refusal to act would undermine the credibility of America's other security commitments, including the President's commitment to prevent Iran from acquiring a nuclear weapon. The word of the United States must mean something. It is vital currency in foreign relations and international and allied commitments.

Every witness here today—Secretary Kerry, General Dempsey, and myself—has served in uniform, fought in war, and seen its ugly realities up close, as has already been noted, Senator McCain. We understand that a country faces few decisions as grave as using military force. We are not unaware of the costs and ravages of war. But we also understand that America must protect its people and its national interests. That is our highest responsibility.

All of us who have the privilege and responsibility of serving this great Nation, owe the American people, and especially those wearing the uniform of our country, vigorous debate on how America should respond to this horrific chemical weapons attack in Syria. I know everyone on this committee agrees and takes their responsibility of office just as seriously as the President and everyone sitting at this table.

Thank you, Mr. Chairman.

[The prepared statement of Secretary Hagel follows:]

PREPARED STATEMENT OF SECRETARY OF DEFENSE CHUCK HAGEL

Chairman Menendez, Ranking Member Corker, thank you for convening this hearing.

In the coming days, Congress will debate how to respond to the most recent chemical weapons attack in Syria—a large-scale, and heinous, sarin gas assault perpetrated by the Syrian government against its own people.

As a former Senator and member of this committee, I welcome this debate and I strongly support President Obama's decision to seek congressional authorization for the use of force in Syria.

As each of us knows, committing the country to using military force is the most difficult decision America's leaders can make. All of those who are privileged to serve our nation have a responsibility to ask tough questions before that commitment is made. The American people must be assured that their leaders are acting according to U.S. national interests, with well-defined military objectives, and with an understanding of the risks and consequences involved.

The President, along with his entire national security team, asked those tough questions before we concluded that the United States should take military action against Syrian regime targets. I want to address how we reached this decision by clarifying the U.S. interests at stake, our military objectives, and the risks of not acting at this critical juncture.

As President Obama said, the use of chemical weapons in Syria is not only an assault on humanity—it is a serious threat to America's national security interests and those of our closest allies.

The Syrian regime's use of chemical weapons poses grave risks to our friends and partners along Syria's borders—including Israel, Jordan, Turkey, Lebanon and Iraq. If Assad is prepared to use chemical weapons against his own people, we have to be concerned that terrorist groups like Hezbollah, which has forces in Syria supporting the Assad regime, could acquire them. This risk of chemical weapons proliferation poses a direct threat to our friends and partners, and to U.S. personnel in the region. We cannot afford for Hezbollah or any terrorist group determined to strike the United States to have incentives to acquire or use chemical weapons.

The Syrian regime's actions risk eroding the nearly century-old international norm against the use of chemical weapons—a norm that has helped protect the United States homeland and American forces operating across the globe from these terrible weapons. Weakening this norm could embolden other regimes to acquire or use chemical weapons. For example, North Korea maintains a massive stockpile of chemical weapons that threatens our treaty ally, the Republic of Korea, and the 28,000 U.S. troops stationed there. I have just returned from Asia, where I had a very serious and long conversation with South Korea's Defense Minister about the threat that North Korea's stockpile of chemical weapons presents to them. Our allies throughout the world must be assured that the United States will fulfill its security commitments.

Given these threats to our national security, the United States must demonstrate through our actions that the use of chemical weapons is unacceptable.

The President has made clear that our military objectives in Syria would be to hold the Assad regime accountable, degrade its ability to carry out these kinds of attacks, and deter the regime from further use of chemical weapons.

The Department of Defense has developed military options to achieve these objectives, and we have positioned U.S. assets throughout the region to successfully execute this mission. We believe we can achieve them with a military action that would be limited in duration and scope.

General Dempsey and I have assured the President that U.S. forces will be ready to act whenever the President gives the order. We are also working with our allies and partners in this effort. Key partners, including France, Turkey, Saudi Arabia, the United Arab Emirates, and other friends in the region, have assured us of their strong support for U.S. action.

In defining our military objectives, we have made clear that we are not seeking to resolve the underlying conflict in Syria through direct military force. Instead we are contemplating actions that are tailored to respond to the use of chemical weapons. A political solution created by the Syrian people is the only way to ultimately end the violence in Syria, and Secretary Kerry is leading international efforts to help the parties in Syria move towards a negotiated transition. We are also committed to doing more to assist the Syrian opposition. But Assad must be held accountable for using these weapons in defiance of the international community.Having defined America's interests and our military objectives, we also must examine the risks and consequences of action, as well as the consequences of inaction.

There are always risks in taking action, but there are also risks with inaction. The Assad regime, under increasing pressure by the Syrian opposition, could feel empowered to carry out even more devastating chemical weapons attacks. Chemical weapons make no distinction between combatants and innocent civilians, and inflict the worst kind of indiscriminate suffering, as we have recently seen.

A refusal to act would undermine the credibility of America's other security commitments—including the President's commitment to prevent Iran from acquiring a nuclear weapon. The word of the United States must mean something. It is vital currency in foreign relations and international and allied commitments.

Every witness here today—Secretary Kerry, General Dempsey, and myself—has served in uniform, fought in war, and seen its ugly realities up close. We understand that a country faces few decisions as grave as using military force. We are not unaware of the costs and ravages of war. But we also understand that America must protect its people and its national interests. That is our highest responsibility.

All of us who have the privilege and responsibility of serving this great nation owe the American people, and especially those wearing the uniform of our country, a vigorous debate on how America should respond to the horrific chemical weapons attack in Syria. I know everyone on this committee agrees, and takes their responsibility of office just as seriously as the President and everyone at this table.

Thank you.

The CHAIRMAN. Thank you, Secretary Hagel. And I know that General Dempsey is available to answer questions from the members of the committee. And in that regard, let me start of by urging members, tomorrow there will be an intelligence briefing for the committee on both the issues at hand, as well as potential military action. So in this setting, we are obviously somewhat constrained about what we might discuss with greater specificity tomorrow.

Mr. Secretary, you make, and have made, a compelling case, and I think it is important, and I appreciate you reiterating the high degree of confidence that exists in our intelligence assessments. I think those are conditions precedent to be able to move forward.

This weekend, I was at a soccer tournament, and I had a group of moms come up to me and say, "Senator, we saw those pictures. They are horrific. We cannot imagine the devastation those parents must feel about their children. But why us? Why us?" And so, I ask you, would you tell them that we would be more secure or less secure by the actions that are being considered, actions for which the President has asked for the authorization of the use of force?

Secretary KERRY. Senator, I would say unequivocally that the President's actions will make us more secure, less likely that Assad can use his weapons or chooses to use his weapons. And the absence of taking the action the President has asked for will, in fact, be far more threatening and dangerous, and potentially ultimately cost lives.

The CHAIRMAN. And do you consider the consequences of inaction greater than the consequences of action?

Secretary KERRY. I do.

The CHAIRMAN. General Dempsey, what do we see as the result of this military campaign, in broad terms of its effect? What do we expect to see at the end of any authorized action; what do we think the results will look like? What is our expectation?

General DEMPSEY. Yes, thank you, Mr. Chairman. The task I have been given is to develop military options to deter; that is to say, change the regime's calculus about the use of chemical weapons, and degrade his ability to do so; that is to say, both activities directly related to chemical weapons themselves, but also to the means of employing them. And anything beyond that, I would prefer to speak about it in a classified setting.

The CHAIRMAN. I understand that. Let me ask you this. In the process of achieving those two goals that you just outlined, would there not be a collateral consequence to the regime of further degrading its overall capabilities?

General DEMPSEY. Yes.

The CHAIRMAN. Mr. Secretary, we received from the administration a proposed resolution for the authorization of force. And, of course, that is a negotiation between the Congress and the administration. Would you tell us whether you believe that a prohibition for having American boots on the ground is something that the administration would accept as part of a resolution?

Secretary KERRY. Mr. Chairman, it would be preferable not to, because there is no intention, or any plan, or any desire whatsoever, to have boots on the ground. I think the President will give you every assurance in the world, as am I, as is the Secretary of Defense, and General Dempsey. But in the event Syria imploded, for instance, or in the event there was a threat of a chemical weapons cache falling into the hands of al-Nusra or someone else, and it was clearly in the interest of our allies and all of us—the British, the French, and others—to prevent those weapons of mass destruction falling into the hands of the worst elements—I do not want to take off the table an option that might or might not be available to the President of the United States to secure our country. So that was the only kind of example—it is the only thing I can think of that would immediately leap to mind to say, no.

The CHAIRMAN. Well, if we said that there would be no troops on the ground for combat purposes, that clearly, I assume—

Secretary KERRY. Well, assuming that in the going to protect those weapons, whether or not they have to, you know, answer a shot in order to be secure, I do not want to speak to that.

The bottom line is this—can I give you the bottom line?

The CHAIRMAN. We are going to have to work to find—

Secretary KERRY. I am absolutely confident, Mr. Chairman, that it is easy, not that complicated, to work out language that will satisfy the Congress and the American people that there is no door open here through which someone can march in ways that the Congress does not want it to while still protecting the national security interests of the country. I am confident that could be worked out.

The CHAIRMAN. Well, I—

Secretary KERRY. The bottom line is, the President has no intention, and will not, and we do not want to, put American troops on the ground to fight this or be involved in the fighting of the civil war period.

The CHAIRMAN. I appreciate that, and I appreciate the response about chemical weapons and the possibility of securing them in our national security interests, as well as our allies. But I do think we are going to have to work on language that makes it clear that this is an overriding issue that I think members, as well as the American people, want to know.

Let me ask you, what—you mentioned it in your remarks. What do you think is the calculus of Iran, North Korea, if we fail to act? And what is the calculus of our allies if we fail to act?

Secretary KERRY. Well, if we fail to act, we are going to have fewer allies. I think we are going to have fewer people who count on us—certainly in the region. We have huge doubts right now. I hear them. I mean, you know, I have the privilege of talking with many of the leaders of these countries with respect to what they may or may not be inclined to do. I have heard their warnings very clearly about what is at stake, not just for them, but for us, in the region. And I think that it is fair to say that our interests would be seriously set back in many respects if we are viewed as not capable—or willing, most important—to follow through on the things that we say matter to us.

As I said earlier in my testimony, this really is not President Obama's red line. The President drew a line that anyone should draw with respect to this convention that we have signed, and which has been in place since the horrors of World War I. And the truth is that through all of World War II, through Vietnam, through Korea, through both Gulf wars, through Afghanistan, through Iraq, the combatants in those efforts have never resorted to this use.

So I think that it is clear, with those prior usages that I referred to, that we would be opening Pandora's box with respect to a whole set of dangerous consequences as a result of the United States not keeping its word. And it would make our life very, very difficult with North Korea and Iran.

There is no question in my mind that those countries are watching, the mullahs and many others are watching what we are doing now with great interest. And that is why even the quality of this debate, and the nature of this debate, are very important.

The CHAIRMAN. Thank you.

Senator Corker.

Senator CORKER. Thank you, Mr. Chairman. And again, thank you for your testimony.

I want to first thank you for bringing this to Congress. I think our foreign policy through the years has been far too focused on the administration. I do not think Congress has played the role that it should play in foreign policy, and I want to thank you for bringing it here and giving us the opportunity to have this debate in advance.

I want to focus a little bit on our strategy with the vetted opposition. I do not know how anybody—as a matter of fact, I know of no one—who has been to the area and spent time with opposition that is not incredibly dismayed by the lack of progress that is occurring there. I know there is a lot of capacity that has to be built. I know there are interagency discussions about whether we should move to industrial-strength training, move away from the kind of activities that are taking place now to build capacity more quickly.

And I just would like, for whichever one of you wants to respond, to talk with us, those of us who have been to the region, who do believe that Syria is important, who are watching what is happening in Iraq as this sectarian issue moves there. It is moving into Lebanon. It is moving; it is certainly destabilizing Jordan.

Why have we been so slow, so inept in so many ways at helping build capacity of this opposition that we have said publicly that we support?

Secretary KERRY. Well, Senator, it is a worthy and important question.

I have had a number of different meetings with the opposition over the course of the months now, since I came in, in February, beginning with a meeting in Rome, and subsequently in Istanbul, and in Amman, Jordan. And the opposition, one has to remember that as little as a year ago there was no great clarity as to the structure of that opposition or even who they were, and they certainly had had no experience in this kind of an endeavor.

Over the course of that year, they have evolved, I would say, significantly. Are they where they need to be? Not completely, but they have changed markedly over the course of the last few months.

At our insistence—and when I say "our" insistence, the insistence of all of their supporters, the so-called "London 11"—they reached out and expanded significantly their base within Syria. They elected new leadership. They brought in a much broader base of Syrian representation including women, including minorities, Christians, others. And so, they have built up a much more competent leadership.

Senator CORKER. If I could, I have only got a few minutes.

Secretary KERRY. Okay.

Senator CORKER. I am very aware of all those things. What I am unaware of is why it is so slow in actually helping them with lethal support? Why has that been so slow?

Secretary KERRY. I think, Senator, we need to have that discussion tomorrow in classified session. We can talk about some components of that. Suffice it to say that it is increasing significantly. I want General Dempsey to speak to this, maybe Secretary Hagel as well. It has increased in its competency. I think it has made leaps and bounds over the course of the last few months.

Secretary Hagel, do you, or General, do you want to?

Secretary HAGEL. I would only add that it was June of this year that the President made the decision to support lethal assistance to the opposition. As you all know, we have been very supportive with hundreds of millions of dollars of nonlethal assistance.

The vetting process, as Secretary Kerry noted, has been significant, but I will ask General Dempsey if he wants to add anything. But we, the Department of Defense, have not been directly involved in this. This is, as you know, a covert action and as Secretary Kerry noted, to go into much more detail would require a closed or classifiedhearing.

General Dempsey?

Senator CORKER. As he is answering that, if he could be fairly brief. Is there anything about the authorization that you are asking that in any way takes away from our stated strategy of empowering the vetted opposition to have the capacity over time to join-in with a transition government as we have stated from the beginning? Is there anything about this authorization that in any way supplements that?

General DEMPSEY. To your question about the opposition, moderate opposition, the path to the resolution of the Syrian conflict is through a developed, capable, moderate opposition, and we know how to do that.

Secondly, there is nothing in this resolution that would limit what we are doing now, but we are very focused on the response to the chemical weapons. I think that subsequent to that, we would probably return to have a discussion about what we might do with the moderate opposition in a more overt way.

Senator CORKER. So, you know, I am very sympathetic to the issue of chemical warfare, and very sympathetic to what this means for U.S. credibility, and I am very sympathetic to the fact that people are watching in the region, and this will have an impact.

But I want to say, I am not sympathetic regarding the lack of effort that has taken place, in my opinion, on the ground as it relates to the vetted opposition. And I hope the end state, that you imagine here, is something that—while it will be proportional and will be surgical—is something that enhances the strategy that we have already laid in place. And I hope you will answer that yes or no, at this time.

General DEMPSEY. The answer to whether I support additional support for the moderate opposition is yes.

Senator CORKER. And this authorization will support those activities in addition to responding to the weapons of mass destruction?

General DEMPSEY. I do not know how the resolution will evolve, but I support those—

Senator CORKER. But what you are seeking. What is it you are seeking?

General DEMPSEY. I cannot answer that, what we are seeking.

Secretary KERRY. The action, if it is authorized, the answer is, as I said in my opening comments, that a consequence of degrading his chemical capacity inevitably will also have a downstream impact on his military capacity.

Senator CORKER. And is this only, this authorization, is only about weapons of mass destruction?

Secretary KERRY. That is correct. This authorization is a limited, targeted effort to focus on deterring and degrading the chemical weapons capacity of the Assad regime.

Senator CORKER. Is that against any other enemies other than the Assad regime?

Secretary KERRY. No, Senator.

Senator CORKER. Is it to be utilized in any other country except inside Syria?

Secretary KERRY. No, Senator.

Senator CORKER. I will say that, in response to your answer to Senator Menendez, I did not find that a very appropriate response regarding boots on the ground. And I do want to say that that is an important element to me, and I hope that as we together work through this, we work through something that is much clearer than the answer that you gave.

While we all feel the actions by the Assad regime are reprehensible, I do not think there are any of us here that are willing to support the possibility of having combat boots on the ground.

Secretary KERRY. Well—

Senator CORKER. And I do hope as we move through this, the administration can be very clear in that regard.

Secretary KERRY. Well, let me be very clear now, because I do not want anything coming out of this hearing that leaves any door open to any possibility. So let's shut that door now as tight as we can.

All I did was raise a hypothetical question about some possibility, and I am thinking out loud about how to protect America's interests. But if you want to know whether there is any, you know, the answer is whatever prohibition clarifies it to Congress and the American people, there will not be American boots on the ground with respect to the civil war.

Senator CORKER. Thank you.

The CHAIRMAN. Thank you.

Senator Boxer.

Senator BOXER. Mr. Chairman and Senator Corker, thank you so much for holding this hearing on a vote of conscience. And I ask unanimous consent that my full statement be entered into the record.

The CHAIRMAN. Without objection.

[The prepared statement of Senator Boxer follows:]

PREPARED STATEMENT OF SENATOR BARBARA BOXER

Mr. Chairman and Senator Corker-thank you for holding this hearing on a vote of conscience in reaction to Syria's use of chemical weapons against its own people.

The images of children gasping for air and young bodies lined up row by row should shock the conscience of the world.

Failure to act could give license to the Syrian President to use these weapons again and send a terrible signal to other brutal regimes like North Korea, which possesses a chemical weapons stockpile.

Since I came to the Senate I voted against the 2003 Iraq War, but I did vote for the use of force against Osama bin Laden in 2001. I did vote to support military missile and air strikes against Serbia in 1999, but I opposed the military surge in Afghanistan in 2009.

I approach this Syria issue in the same way that I approached those—with a heavy heart and an independent mind.

I have heard some of my colleagues compare President Obama's position on Syria to the decision to invade Iraq in 2003.

This is a false comparison.

In Iraq, the Bush administration was trying to prove the existence of an active weapons of mass destruction program in a country where such a program did not exist.

Here, we know that Assad has stockpiles of chemical weapons.

In Iraq, the Bush administration was preparing to invade and occupy a country with well over 100,000 U.S. troops.

In this case, the President has been clear: No ground invasion. No occupation. No comparison between Iraq and Syria.

So why should we take targeted action against Syria?

Because allowing the continued use of chemical weapons to go unanswered makes it more likely that terrorists could obtain and use them on America or our allies, including Israel. And it makes it more likely that Iran will view us as a paper tiger when it comes to their nuclear program.

In 1997, the Senate supported a ban on chemical weapons by a vote of 74-26.

I voted to approve the Chemical Weapons Convention because chemical weapons have no place in the civilized world and some behavior must be out of bounds. Shouldn't an overwhelming vote like this mean something? Shouldn't the Senate stand behind its words and actions?

In 2003, we passed the Syria Accountability Act by a vote of 89-4—legislation that I introduced which states that Syria's ''acquisition of weapons of mass destruction ... threatens the security of the Middle East and the national security interests of the United States.''

Shouldn't an overwhelming vote like this mean something? Shouldn't the Senate stand behind its words and actions?

Not only has our President drawn a red line on the use of chemical weapons, so did the Senate with the passage of the Syria Accountability Act and ratification of the Chemical Weapons Convention.

I know there is tremendous reluctance to get involved in another military effort and sometimes the easiest thing to do when others suffer is to walk away. Well, I don't believe we should close our eyes to this clear violation of long-standing international norms. I believe America's morality, America's reputation, and America's credibility are on the line.

I applaud President Obama for coming to Congress and will support a targeted response to Syria's unspeakable deeds to gas its own people to death.

Senator BOXER. So I am going to make a brief statement because a lot of people have been asking me how I view this, including my own constituents. And then I will ask some questions about the intel, if I can.

Mr. Chairman, thank you for showing us those images of children because even though it is really hard to look at, we have to look at it. Children gasping for air, young bodies lined up in a row should shock the world.

And the failure to act, I think, gives license to the Syrian President to use these weapons again. And it sends a terrible signal to other brutal regimes, like North Korea. And can I thank you, Secretary Hagel, for bringing up the issue of North Korea in your opening statement, and you, Secretary Kerry, for bringing it up? I mean, how many of us have been there to the line where we see thousands of our troops standing there, just a stone's throw away from North Korea? We need to think about it. Maybe because I am from California, I tend to look at Asia, but this is very serious. We see that danger up close when we go to that line.

Now, since I came to the Senate, I voted against the Iraq war, but I did vote for the use of force against Osama bin Laden. I voted to support air strikes against Serbia, but I vocally opposed the military surge in Afghanistan. So I approach this Syria issue in the same way I approached those: With a very heavy heart and a very independent mind.

I have heard some of my colleagues compare President Obama's position on Syria to the decision to invade Iraq in 2003, and I thank Secretary Kerry for discussing this because I believe it is a totally false comparison. And I know it has been mentioned before; you drew that line again.

In Iraq, the Bush administration prepared to invade and occupy a country with well over 100,000 U.S. troops. In this case, the President has been clear: no ground invasion. No occupation. We will have that in our resolution.

So why should we take any targeted action against Syria? Not only is it important to keep North Korea in mind, but also allowing the continued use of chemical weapons to go unanswered, makes it much more likely that we will see them used again in Syria, and we will see them used maybe elsewhere. And terrorists could obtain those chemical weapons and use them on America, or our allies, or our troops. Use them, for example, against Israel and other friends. It makes it more likely—and this is key—that Iran will view us as a paper tiger when it comes to their nuclear program, and that is dangerous, not only for us and our friends, but for the world.

Now, in 1997, the Senate supported a ban on chemical weapons by a vote of 74 to 26. Should not an overwhelming vote like that mean something? Should not the Senate stand behind its words and actions? And then, in 2003, we passed the Syria Accountability Act by a vote of 89 to 4. I wrote that bill with Senator Santorum. We had a huge vote in favor of it. This is what it says, "acquisition of weapons of mass destruction ... threatens the security of the Middle East and the national security interests of the United States." Should not an overwhelming vote like that meant something? Should not the Senate stand behind its words and its actions?

So, I believe, as Secretary Kerry said, and I will reiterate it, that not only has our President drawn a line, a red line, on the use of chemical weapons, and not only has the world done so, but we, in the Senate, we did so.

Now, I know there is tremendous reluctance to get involved in another military effort. And sometimes the easiest thing to do is to walk away. Well, I believe we cannot close our eyes to this clear violation of longstanding international norms. I believe America's morality, America's reputation, and America's credibility are on the line.

I applaud this administration and our President for coming to Congress. I applaud those who asked him to come to Congress. It is the right thing to do, and I will support a targeted effort, but not a blank check, to respond to Syria's unspeakable deeds to gas its own people to death.

Now, my question involves the intel here, and I do not know how much you can give us, so I am going to try to make this pretty broad, so you can answer it, and whomever feels most comfortable.

A lot of people are fearful, because of what happened in Iraq, that there might be some disagreement between the intelligence agencies, and we have a lot of intelligence agencies, 17 in all. I do not know how many were involved in this, whether it was four, or six, or eight. I do not know whether you can disclose that.

But my question is: Was there any argument about this fact, that they agree that there is high confidence that these weapons were used by the Assad regime? Was there any debate? I mean, there was debate. Was there any dissension between the various agencies?

Secretary KERRY. The intelligence community, represented by DNI Clapper, has released a public document, unclassified, available for all to see, in which they make their judgment with high confidence that the facts are as they have set forth. So, I think that speaks for itself.

Senator BOXER. Well, I am going to press just a little bit harder here, John, Mr. Secretary, if I can.

Out of all the different agencies, because I remember in Iraq, sure, eventually the word came down, everyone agreed, but then we found out there was disagreement.

To your knowledge, did they all come to the same conclusion, the various intelligence agencies?

Secretary KERRY. To my knowledge, I have no knowledge of any agency that was a dissenter, or anybody who had an alternative theory. And I do know, I think it is safe to say, that they had a whole team that ran a scenario to try to test their theory, to see if there was any possibility they could come up with an alternative view as to who might have done it. And the answer is: They could not.

Senator BOXER. Okay. Last question on intel and Russia. I read—and I do not know if this is true or false, but I read in one of the publications today that members of the Russian parliament were going to come here to lobby our colleagues, to tell our colleagues, that there is no such intelligence, that there is no proof. I, myself, met with the Russian Ambassador several times on this matter, and I knew right away, a long time ago, they were going to do nothing to help us.

But what are they clinging to here? How could they make that case given what you have said?

Secretary KERRY. I, honestly, I do not know. I mean, there is no way for me to hang my hat on what it is. I think that—I have had personal conversations with the foreign minister. They make an argument to some effect that we do not have evidence, and that the opposition did it. No matter what you show, that is the argument they take. Now, as to why they do that or what the rationale is, I am not going to speculate.

The President, as you know, is leaving this evening to go to St. Petersburg for the summit. He will have ample opportunity to hear firsthand from President Putin, and I am confident they will have a discussion about it.

Senator BOXER. Thank you.

The CHAIRMAN. Senator Risch.

Senator RISCH. Thank you, Mr. Chairman.

Secretary KERRY. Could I just say? I want to add, though. I think it is important for us not to get into an unnecessary struggle over some of this with the Russians for a lot of reasons.

The Russians are working with us and cooperating on this effort to try to make a negotiated process work. And I think they are serious about trying to find the way forward with that, number one.

Number two, on major issues like START, North Korea, Iran, the Russians are cooperating. So I think, you know, we have to sort of deal with this thoughtfully, and let us hope that the summit might produce some change of heart as the President makes the evidence available to President Putin.

Senator BOXER. Thank you.

The CHAIRMAN. Senator.

Senator RISCH. Mr. Chairman, first of all, let me say that I have seen the pictures of what happened, and I have been seeing pictures for 14 months or more; 2 years, I guess, of what is going on over there. You cannot have an ounce of compassion in you and not be moved tremendously by what is happening there. It is awful. It is horrendous.

There has been almost 100,000 people killed there, and we all know, I guess, in an unclassified setting, we can say that these people have used gas on multiple occasions, but the deaths have only been in the hundreds and not in the thousands. But all of this is moving, and there is no question about it.

Nonetheless, I am reluctant. If this was one American, if this was an attack against any American, against any American interest, this would be a no-brainer for me. But I am reluctant at this point, and part of it stems from where this is going to go as to the limit we are going to put on it.

Secretary Kerry, you said you have met with your counterpart from Russia. First of all, you say they are cooperating with us on all major issues. I view this as a major issue, and I do not view them as cooperating with us. They are printing their currency. They are providing them with information. They are providing them with technology. They have provided them with a tremendous amount of military power.

And so, the question I have is: What is your counterpart telling you as to what they are going to do when, and if, America pulls the trigger?

Secretary KERRY. Senator, look, I understand anybody's reluctance about this. But again, I would ask you to confront the greater reality of what happens if we do not do something. I mean, if you think it is bad today what they are doing, just think about what happens if they confirm their suspicion that the United States is not going to do anything.

One of the reasons Assad has been using these materials is because they have, up until now, made the calculation that the West—writ large, and the United States particularly—are not going to do anything about it. Impunity is already working to kill a lot of people, and to make things more dangerous, and I guarantee you that is in their assessment.

So if we make it worse by not being willing to do something, those terrible images you see are going to be worse. But worse than that, our interests will be setback: Israel will be at greater risk. Jordan will be at greater risk. The longer that this conflict goes on, and particularly with Assad's ability to be able to use chemical weapons, the more you will see the humanitarian crisis grow.

We are already the largest contributor, thanks to the generosity of the American people and the willingness of Congress to move. We are already the largest contributor to refugee camps in the borders, and many of you have been to them. Do you want to see them grow? Do you want to see Jordan, which is already fragile?

Senator RISCH. Of course, not.

Secretary KERRY. Many of you have met with the King. You know King Abdullah's judgment is that he is at-risk because of what is happening. So I believe the best way to curb that and reduce the threat is by acting.

Senator RISCH. And I do not disagree with anything you said, but let us take that, and try to expand on that.

We need the credibility, there is no question about it, but are we really going to be giving them credibility? If we go in with a limited strike, and the day after, or the week after, or the month after, Assad crawls out of his rat hole and says, ''Look. I stood up to the strongest power on the face of this earth, and I won. And so, now it is business as usual here.''

And he may say, ''And by the way, I am not going to use chemical weapons anymore because I do not like what just happened, but I am going to continue to use conventional weapons.'' And we are going to go on with business as usual, and the refugees are going to continue, and the thousands are going to be killed. And our allies are going to say, ''What is the matter with you, United States? You said you would do something about this. You did a limited strike, but you did not finish Assad off and the problem is just as bad as it was.''

What does that do to our credibility? You know, that concerns me.

Secretary KERRY. Well, Senator, let me speak to that. It is a good question.

First of all, I think General Dempsey will tell you, Assad may be able to crawl out of the hole and say, ''Look, I survived.'' But there is no way that with reality, and other assessments, he is going to be able to say he is better off.

There is no question that—whatever choices are made by the President—that Assad, and his military effort, will not be better off, number one. And the opposition will know that, and the people in Syria will know that.

Already today, just with the threat that action may be taken, defections have gone up, and people in Syria are reconsidering whether Assad is a long-term bet.

Moreover, General Dempsey has made it clear, and Secretary Hagel has made it clear, and the President has made it clear, that there will be additional support to the opposition, which is only now in its third month of receiving the overt support—or about to receive, in fairness, as Senator McCain and others know—there are things that have not gotten there yet. But that process is in place and that will increase. So I believe—

Senator RISCH. My time is almost up, Secretary.

I really want to get a handle on this. I think all of us feel strongly about this, and I need to be reassured on this. The other thing that just really troubles me about this is: What happens if this thing gets away from us? What happens? You have been on the border between Israel and Lebanon, as I have. And since the last war, I mean they have, Hezbollah has really beefed that up.

What happens if they get into it with Israel? What is our response to that going to be?

Secretary KERRY. Well, I talked with Prime Minister Netanyahu just yesterday, and he made it pretty clear to me that Israel feels very confident about Israel's ability to deal, as they have previously, with a miscalculation by Assad.

And the rest of the community—the Turks, the Jordanians, the Emirates, the Saudis, the Qataris, the United States, France, others—all have a capacity.

So as I said in my statement, you all have to make a calculation here just as Assad does. If he is foolish enough to respond to the world's enforcement against his criminal activity, if he does, he will invite something far worse, and I believe, something absolutely unsustainable for him. Now, that does not mean the United States of America is going to war. As I said in my comments, there are plenty of options here.

Senator RISCH. Well, we do know—

Secretary KERRY. Let me finish; one other comment because it is important to the earlier question. Russia does not have an ideological commitment here. This is a geopolitical, transactional commitment. And our indications are, in many regards, that that is the way they view it. There may be more weapons to sell as a result of weapons sold, but it is not going to elicit some kind of major confrontation. Now, let me go further.

They have condemned the use of chemical weapons; the Russians have. The Iranians have. And as the proof of the use becomes even clearer in the course of this debate, I think it is going to be very difficult for Iran or Russia to decide against all of that evidence that there is something worth defending here.

So this is the kind of calculation you have to make, but I would measure that against the calculation of what happens if we do not respond. If we do not respond, we are going to be back here asking you to respond to some greater confrontation with greater potential for damage and danger because somebody miscalculated as a result of believing the United States is not good for what it says. And that will invite much greater danger to the American people, much greater risk for our armed forces, and conceivably, much greater chances of a genuine kind of conflagration that we do not want to see.

Senator RISCH. Thank you, Mr. Chairman. My time is up. Thank you, Secretary.

The CHAIRMAN. Senator Cardin.

Senator CARDIN. Well, let me thank all of you for being here, but also thank you very much for your service. And Mr. Chairman and Senator Corker, I thank you very much for arranging this hearing.

It is very clear, the type of conduct that President Assad has done in Syria, his actions have created a humanitarian crisis, and now he has escalated to the use of chemical weapons. The evidence has been presented, and it is clear that we have to respond, and a military response is justified. So I support your efforts.

And, Mr. Secretary, the way that you have described it is what I think we need to do. We have to have a tailored mission that deals with degrading and deterring the use of chemical weapons. We need to have it focused on that mission. It has got to be done in a way that protects civilians the best that we can. And it has got to be of very limited duration.

But I just want to come back to the point that the Chairman raised and your own comments, where you say we should shut that door as tightly as possible when dealing with putting our troops on the ground in Syria.

I have read the resolution that you presented to us. I think it is broader than what you have stated as the President's intentions on the mission, and I understand that. And I understand the President's strong desire to keep the mission very tight. And it certainly does not close the door on the introduction of ground troops.

I have also heard your comments about the unexpected, something could happen. I would just point out that the President, as Commander-in-Chief, has the authority, the inherent authority, to act in urgent situations where time requires that action. And I would suggest that as you have come to Congress for this authorization, if circumstances change and there is time to come to Congress, you will have the opportunity to come back to Congress and seek our participation. We are a separate branch of government, as you recall.

So I just want to urge you in the strongest possible terms to work with our leadership to draft a resolution that is as tight as we can make it to allow you to carry out the mission that you have defined here today. So that we can go back and tell the American people that we, in Congress, are supporting your action, but are not leaving open the door for the introduction of American troops into Syria.

I want to talk a little bit about the specific military operations, and I am going to leave most of this for tomorrow in our discussions. Have you put into that equation the fact that obviously Syria is aware that we are contemplating military action and therefore may try to change the equation during this period of time to make it more difficult for us to carry out that mission? Has that been brought into your planning stages?

General DEMPSEY. Yes, Senator, it has. And time works both ways. You recall about a week and a half ago there was a significant leak of military planning that caused the regime to react. So, time works both ways. We have some pretty significant intelligence capabilities, and we continue to refine our targets.

Senator CARDIN. Both of you have indicated your concern about American military involvement in Syria, that it could draw us into an internal conflict. Are you also putting into your plans ways to prevent America being drawn into the internal conflict in Syria?

Secretary HAGEL. Senator, we are. As I noted in my opening statement, we have taken great care and much time in looking at all of not only the options to present to the President but the contingencies that may be a consequence of the President selecting one of those options, including what you have just noted. It is imperfect, as I said, and I think everyone recognizes there is always risk. We have tried to minimize that risk in every way we can in every presentation we have made to the President. The President has insisted on that, minimal collateral damage across the board.

So, yes, we have taken a lot of time to focus exactly on your point.

Senator CARDIN. Secretary Kerry, you point out that if we don't act, we are liable to lose some friends. And I want to point out that we have a direct interest here. We not only have humanitarian reasons to respond to the use of chemical weapons, we have a direct American interest in that region, and we have Americans that are in that region that are at risk if additional chemicals are used. So, I see a direct connection to U.S. interests.

You say we might lose some friends if we don't act. Why don't we have more participation in the U.S. military response in addition to just support? It seems to me that America will be in the lead, but it does not seem like we have a growing list of countries that are actively joining us in the military operation.

Secretary KERRY. Well, first of all, there is no definitive list at this point in time because the President has not made the decision as to specifically which set of choices he is going to operate on.

Secondly, as many countries as we could conceivably need to be able to be helpful in a limited operation have volunteered to be helpful, and they stand ready to take part in any specific operation, and we are very comfortable with that.

But the bottom line in many ways remains that we are talking about very specific kinds of capacities that in some cases only the United States of America possesses. And so that remains open. It is a process that will evolve as this debate evolves and as the President makes his decisions and the Joint Chiefs of Staff and the military present him with the various options, and those will probably evolve as you mentioned. People may make adjustments in Syria, and I can assure the Syrians that General Dempsey and his people are making adjustments as they go along.

Senator CARDIN. Well, I would hope we would have stronger international participation. Is there a consideration of a role for NATO to play here, considering that one of NATO's partners, Turkey, is on the direct front line? Is that being considered?

Secretary KERRY. Well, as you say, is it being considered, everything is being considered, and all of these things are being evaluated. Discussions are taking place. I will be meeting on Saturday in Vilnius with the European ministers. I know this topic will come up, and most of them, they are all members of NATO, or most of them are, not all of them. So we will have some discussions when we are there.

But at the moment, this is a limited operation with the scope of support that the President makes a judgment that we ought to have. We will have very broad—we have already very broad—we have had some 53 nations or countries and organizations acknowledge that chemical weapons were used here and have condemned it publicly. Thirty-one nations have stated publicly that the Assad regime is responsible, and I think we are at about 34 countries have indicated that if the allegations are true, that they would support some form of action against Syria.

So there is a very broad coalition that is growing of people who believe we ought to take action against Syria, but the question is whether or not it makes sense. For whatever number to be part of it is a decision that our military and the President have to make as we go along here.

Senator CARDIN. I will reserve the rest of the questions for the closed session. Thank you.

The CHAIRMAN. Senator Rubio?

[Audience Disruption.]

The CHAIRMAN. The gentleman will sit down or I will have the officer remove you.

The police will make sure that the committee is in order.

Senator Rubio?

Senator RUBIO. Thank you, Mr. Chairman.

Let me begin by answering a fundamental question that I get asked a lot as we discuss this very important issue, and that is why we even care about what is happening in Syria. I want to make very clear my belief that I think reflects the belief of most of the members of this committee, and that is that what happens in Syria is a vital national interest to the United States and to our national security for reasons that have already been outlined.

The Syrian relationship with Iran is very significant. It is a key part of their ambitions to be the regional power, the dominant regional power. In fact, the Iranians love to brag that Syria gives them a border with Israel.

Number two, Assad is an anti-American supporter of terrorism. He is a supporter of Hamas. He is a supporter of Hezbollah. And, by the way, he is a supporter of Al Qaeda in Iraq, the same Al Qaeda in Iraq that is responsible for the death and maiming of countless brave young men and women who served our country in uniform.

It is also of interest to us because of the instability that this is creating in Syria, instability that is allowing portions of Syria to quickly become kind of what Afghanistan was before 9/11, the premier operational space for global jihadists from abroad to come train and fight and plan attacks in the future. And now, added to that is this chemical attack, which undermines the post-World War

II world order which basically said that these things are unacceptable.

And allies that look at the United States and our capabilities of living up to our security promises are all at risk now as a result of all of this.

This is why Syria and what is happening in Syria matters to our national interest, why it is so clearly tied to a critical national security interest to the United States.

By the way, most, if not all of this was true two years ago when I joined other voices on this committee and in the Senate and beyond that advocated that at that time, when Assad was on the ropes, that the United States should engage in trying to identify moderate elements and equip them so that they became the predominant rebel force in Syria and not others.

But that didn't happen. Instead, the choice was made to lead from behind. The choice was made to watch as this thing unfolded. Others advocated that we should just mind our own business, and what we are seeing here now is proof and an example that when America ignores these problems, these problems don't ignore us, that we can ignore them, but eventually they grow and they come to visit us at our doorstep, and now we are faced with what we have.

In fact, Secretary Kerry, a moment ago you said that one of the calculations that Assad used in deciding to use chemical weapons was that the U.S. wouldn't do anything about it. I understand perhaps why he made that calculation because, yes, this was a horrible incident where a thousand people died, but before this incident 100,000 people had died, snipers were used to pick off civilians, women were raped—they were going to these villages and carrying this out, and nothing happened. So, of course he reached that calculation.

So this is a reminder of what happens when we ignore the world, when we look inward sometimes and we ignore these problems. They only get worse and more difficult to solve, and that is the mess that we have here right now. We are left with options, all of which are less than ideal, and I want to walk through the three that have been presented to us by different voices and then ask specifically about the one the President is considering.

The first option is to decide to help Syrians remove Assad and replace him with a more moderate government. I think that is the ideal outcome, but it has its own complications. Today, the rebel forces on the ground are not just the moderate rebels. There are non-moderate rebels. There are jihadists that now control major portions of the country, and other parts of the country are intermingled with these rebel forces, creating a real prospect that after the fall of Assad a new civil war could be triggered, one that could involve sectarian violence, massacres of minorities, et cetera. So this comes with its own set of complications.

The other, which some voices have advocated, is doing nothing, but that would guarantee the following outcome, an emboldened Assad, an emboldened Iran, increased instability in the country because portions of that country will still be ungoverned, and it will also send a message to the world that there is no red line that they should fear crossing. So Iran will move forward toward nuclear weapons. North Korea can act crazier, if that is even possible. Our allies in South Korea and Japan may start to doubt their security arrangements with us. Israel may decide it needs to strike Iran unilaterally. Iran will move toward the bomb, which, by the way, won't just be an Iranian bomb. It will be a Turkish bomb as well, and a Saudi bomb, and maybe even an Egyptian bomb one day.

The third is the action the President is asking us to consider, what he termed—not me—what he called a shot across the bow, a military strike of limited duration and scope that has three goals, as I understand it, that have been outlined here today.

Goal number one is to hold Assad accountable. Goal number two is to deter this behavior in the future. And goal number three is to degrade Assad's capacity to carry out these attacks in the future. This is what the President wants us to authorize, a limited strike that would accomplish these three things.

The questions that I have, quite frankly, I am a bit skeptical that what the President is asking for will provide the support needed to achieve these objectives, and that these objectives are even realistic at this point.

So, here is my first question. I think I will ask this of General Dempsey. The calculation that Assad has made is that the reason why he is using these chemical weapons is because he is afraid that if he doesn't, he could lose this war, be overthrown and killed. That is the calculation that he has made. That is why he used these chemical weapons. He wants to beat the rebels.

Can we structure an attack that tips that calculation where he will basically decide that he would rather risk being overrun by rebels than risk a limited attack from the U.S. if he uses these chemical weapons? He has to decide, I will use chemical weapons and take on a limited U.S. attack in the future, or I will risk being overrun by the rebels.

How are we going to unbalance that and lead him to calculate that he is better off risking losing to the rebels?

General DEMPSEY. Well, Senator, I think it may be even more insidious than that. He has reached a point where he now thinks of chemical weapons as just another weapon in his arsenal, and that is the part that makes this so very dangerous. And I think that as I have provided advice on what targets may be appropriate, I certainly want to degrade his capabilities coming out of this. I want to come out of it stronger than we go into it.

Senator RUBIO. That leads me to my second question. How confident are you, and how confident can you express to this committee that you are, that we can in fact put in place a military plan that is limited in scope and duration that can effectively degrade Assad's capability to carry out future chemical attacks?

General DEMPSEY. I am confident in the capabilities we can bring to bear to deter and degrade, and it won't surprise you to know that we will have not only an initial target set but subsequent target sets should they become necessary.

Senator RUBIO. And this question is probably for Secretary Kerry, and I think this was asked earlier but I think it is important to elaborate on it. One of the concerns that I have, and I have heard others express, is that Assad could take three, five, six days of strikes, maybe longer, maybe shorter, and emerge from that saying I have faced down the United States and I have held onto power and survived, and at that point be further emboldened both domestically and perhaps even abroad.

Have we taken that into account? I understand your argument that inaction would be worse, but have we taken into account what the implications could be of an Assad that could weather a limited strike and what that could mean for the long-term prospects of the conflict?

Secretary KERRY. Yes, we absolutely have. For certain, we have taken that into account. He will weather. I mean, he will weather. The President is asking for a limited authority to degrade his current capacity and to deter him from using it again. He is not asking for permission from the Congress to go destroy the entire regime or to do a much more extensive kind of thing. That is not what he is asking.

So he will be able to stand up, and no doubt he will try to claim that somehow this is something positive for him. But I think General Dempsey has made it clear, and I think we believe deeply, as do others who are knowledgeable about this in the region, that there is no way that it will, in fact, be beneficial for him, that it will not translate for him on the ground, that the defections that are taking place now and other things that will happen will further degrade his capacity to prosecute going forward.

And I want to emphasize something. I want to come back to it because I don't want anybody misinterpreting this from earlier. This authorization does not contemplate and should not have any allowance for any troops on the ground. I just want to make that absolutely clear. What I was doing was hypothesizing about a potential that might occur at some point in time but not in this authorization, in no way. Let me be crystal clear, there is no problem in our having the language that has zero capacity for American troops on the ground within the authorization the President is asking for. I don't want anybody in the media or elsewhere to misinterpret that coming out of here, as I said earlier. I repeat it again now. That is important.

The CHAIRMAN. Thank you. And I can assure you, that will be in the resolution.

Secretary KERRY. Good.

The CHAIRMAN. Senator Shaheen?

Senator SHAHEEN. Thank you, Mr. Chairman.

Thank you, gentlemen, for your testimony. I agree that we should not turn our back on such a blatant violation of international norms with respect to the use of chemical weapons, and that if we stand quietly by while a tyrant like Assad uses chemical weapons on his own people, that we will be giving carte blanche to any dictator anywhere in the world to develop and use chemical weapons.

I think the question now, as we have all said, is how we respond specifically. How do we best send a message that it is completely unacceptable to develop, much less use, these types of weapons, and how do we do that without inadvertently spreading the conflict beyond the borders of Syria? That is really the question that we have today.

We have heard that we want to deter the future use of chemical weapons, but according to the President and from your testimony today, we don't want to tip the scales on the ground. So how do we ensure that we can do that without spreading the conflict throughout the region, and how do we hit Assad hard enough so that we deter his future use of chemical weapons and yet don't affect the military outcome on the ground?

Secretary KERRY. General, do you want to address just the military piece, and I will take the other piece?

General DEMPSEY. Sure. I think the language about not using American military power to tip the scale would be our direct action. In other words, this resolution is not asking for permission for the President to be able to use the United States Armed Forces to overthrow the regime.

On the other hand, back to the earlier questions about developing a moderate regime that has capabilities to be a stabilizing force inside of Syria, that is the path. Our military action in this case is very focused on the chemical weapons but will have the added benefit of degrading, and it will also have the added benefit of supporting the diplomatic track.

And with that, let me turn it over to the secretary.

Secretary KERRY. Senator Shaheen, the President has made it very, very clear that the policy of this administration—and sometimes people have said, have questioned precisely what it is, and I will tell you precisely what it is. The President is asking for the Congress to take steps that will specifically deter and degrade Assad's capacity to use chemical weapons. He is not asking the Congress for authorization to become whole-hog involved in Syria's civil war to try to change the regime through military action. This is a targeted action to deal with the problem of chemical weapons.

But, there is a separate track which the President has already committed the administration and the country to, which is that Assad must go, that he has lost all moral authority or capacity to ever govern Syria, and he is pursuing that, the President is pursuing that track by helping the opposition, by now having made the decision to lethally arm that opposition by upgrading the efforts of the opposition to be able to fight the fight, not the United States, the opposition, and to be able to come to a negotiated settlement because the President is convinced, as I think everybody is, that there is no military solution, that ultimately you want to get to Geneva, you want a negotiated settlement, and under the terms of Geneva One, there is an agreement which the Russians have signed on to which calls for a transition government to be created with the mutual consent of the current regime and the opposition, and that transition government will establish the rules of the road for the Syrian people to choose their new government.

There is no way possible that by mutual consent Assad is going to be part of that future. The Russians have agreed that that is, in fact, Geneva One, and the purpose of the Geneva Two meeting is to implement Geneva One.

Now, it is complicated, obviously. How do you get there? And that is part of this struggle. But the President is convinced that as the support to the opposition increases, there is a much greater likelihood that you will wind up ultimately with a negotiated settlement.

The alternative is that you stand back and do nothing and Syria, in fact, implodes, becomes an enclave state. There are huge ungoverned spaces. Al Nusra, Al Qaeda, Hezbollah, others become more of a threat to our friends in the region, and the region becomes much more of a sectarian conflagration.

Senator SHAHEEN. Thank you, Mr. Secretary.

Secretary Hagel and General Dempsey, you made a number of statements throughout the spring cautioning against intervention in the conflict in Syria. Why do you feel at this point that it is appropriate for us to take action? What has changed?

Secretary HAGEL. Senator, thank you. I will let General Dempsey respond for himself.

Well, first, very clear intelligence and evidence that the Assad regime used chemical weapons on its own people. So, we are dealing with a new set of realities based on facts. And I think it is at least my opinion that that needs to be addressed, that needs to be dealt with for the reasons I have noted, I have said in public and also addressed in my statement, and I think what Secretary Kerry and General Dempsey have said, and obviously what the President has said. So that is the most specific reason. The dynamics have changed.

One additional point in regard to your question on this as to your previous question. If, in fact, the President is given the authorization from Congress to go forward, and as he has already said, he believes he has within his constitutional power as commander-in-chief to act as well, and he has given his reasons, which we all support, why he came to the Congress, there are parallel actions that would work along with whatever action the President would take, which Secretary Kerry has noted: Opposition strength, defections within the Syrian government and military, and other consequences.

And this is about getting to an end game. That end game is a diplomatic settlement. It is driving this toward what the President believes is the only way out of this, if for no other reason than what Secretary Kerry has noted: We do not want to see the country of Syria disintegrate and result in ungoverned space because the consequences would be devastating for our partners, for our allies, and for the entire Middle East. At that point we would all have to respond in some way.

So I would just add that onto answering your last question.

General DEMPSEY. Chairman, may I? I will make it brief.

The CHAIRMAN. Yes, sir.

General DEMPSEY. But in response to your question about, let's say, the past year, over the past year we have provided a full range of options, and my advice on those options was based on my assessment of their linkage to our national security interests and whether they would be effective. On this issue—that is, the use of chemical weapons—I find a clear linkage to our national security interests, and we will find a way to make our use of force effective.

Senator SHAHEEN. Thank you all.

The CHAIRMAN. Senator Johnson?

Senator JOHNSON. Thank you, Mr. Chairman.

I am trying to reconcile the two tracks of goals we have here: military action and a negotiated settlement. Secretary Hagel, you said we are not seeking to resolve the underlying conflict in Syria. Isn't that exactly what we're trying to do? Why aren't we trying to resolve that?

Secretary HAGEL. I was referring in my statement to the authorization to use military force. That specifically is not why we have come to the Congress, why the President asked for the Congress' support. As he has said, the authorization is for a very specific and focused military action.

Senator JOHNSON. But our stated goal really is to remove Assad and move toward a negotiated settlement. Why wouldn't we use this opportunity, the military action, to move toward that goal?

Secretary HAGEL. Well, that is one option, if those options would range from an invasion or a lot of military options on the table. The President has said that this resolution is about a limited authorization for a limited exercise. The goal of removing Assad from office, as the President has stated, is still the policy of this administration.

Senator JOHNSON. General Dempsey, how confident are you that you can calibrate, tailor, and fine-tune military action that doesn't have spillover effects so that we keep it to the limited stated goal of degrading and deterring?

General DEMPSEY. Well, the task was to do just that, to deter and degrade, and to be limited in focus and scope and duration. I mean, that is the task I've been given and the task I have—-

Senator JOHNSON. Yes, but how can you calibrate that?

General DEMPSEY. Well, we can calibrate it on our side. There is always the risk of escalation on the other, but they have significantly limited capabilities to do so, and most of the intelligence informs us—we could talk about that in a closed session.

Senator JOHNSON. What planning is being undertaken right now in case this does spin out of control? We were talking about the potential for boots on the ground.

Secretary Kerry, I am very glad to hear you are bringing into the equation what I think is our number one national security interest, and that is those chemical weapons falling into the hands of Al Qaeda elements or possibly even Hezbollah. What commitment do we have long term to make sure that doesn't happen? If you have a very limited resolution here, how do we know that we will prevent that from happening?

Secretary KERRY. Senator Johnson, this is this moment in time, and as the President said, he is asking for a limited military response, recognizing that neither he nor most of America want to be dragged into a civil war in Syria.

Senator JOHNSON. But our goal is to get rid of Assad.

Secretary KERRY. Our goal is to help the opposition. You have to look overall. The President—and I think all of us agree—I mean, can you imagine Assad running Syria? Can you imagine this man who has gassed his people remaining in power.

Senator JOHNSON. Again, I am trying to reconcile why, if we are going to go in there militarily, if we're going to strike, why wouldn't we try to do some kind of knockout punch? Is it because we simply have no faith that there is anybody on the ground, the rebels, to take—

Secretary KERRY. No. No, absolutely not.

Senator JOHNSON. Or is it not ready for regime change? Is that the problem?

Secretary KERRY. No, Senator, that is not the reason. The reason is that the President is listening to the American people and has made a policy decision, and in addition, that is not something that the United States of America needs to engage in or ought to engage in. That is a much broader operation.

Senator JOHNSON. But it is a stated goal.

Secretary KERRY. Well, yes, it is. It is, Senator. Is the Congress of the United States ready to pay for 30 days of 30,000 airstrikes, and is there a legal justification for doing that? You could run through a whole series of different questions here that are very serious about what you are talking about.

Senator JOHNSON. What do we know about the opposition? Have we been tracking them for the last two years? I mean, it seems like—and this is more of an impression I have as opposed to any exact knowledge—initially the opposition was maybe more Western leaning, more moderate, more democratic, and as time has gone by, it has degraded and become more infiltrated by Al Qaeda. Is that basically true, or to what extent has that happened?

Secretary KERRY. No. That is actually basically not true. It is basically incorrect. The opposition has increasingly become more defined by its moderation, more defined by the breadth of its membership, and more defined by its adherence to a democratic process and to an all-inclusive, minority-protecting constitution which will be broad-based and secular with respect to the future of Syria. That is very critical.

Senator JOHNSON. Secretary Hagel, do you—

Secretary KERRY. Let me just finish one other point about the opposition. It is my understanding, because I talked to the president of the opposition yesterday, he is in Germany now. He is meeting with the German Parliament. He is coming to Great Britain. He will be meeting with Parliament in Great Britain. He is prepared to come here as soon as those meetings are over in order to meet with you, and you can have an opportunity to talk to President Jarber and meet with the opposition, have a much better sense of who they are.

Senator JOHNSON. We appreciate that. Secretary Hagel, do you have a feel for the number of members of the opposition? How large is their force?

Secretary HAGEL. I don't know the numbers. Our intelligence communities have estimates of those numbers. But I think, as Secretary Kerry said, the momentum has shifted in the opinion of our intelligence community and others who are close to the situation.

Senator JOHNSON. I'm kind of a numbers guy. General Dempsey, do you know the force strength of the rebel forces?

General DEMPSEY. I don't have them committed to memory, Senator.

Senator JOHNSON. But we have them. I can give—

General DEMPSEY. Yeah, the intelligence community has that available. We'll make it available tomorrow.

Senator JOHNSON. Do you also have a pretty good feel for how many really would be considered moderate versus the elements of Al Qaeda?

General DEMPSEY. I have seen documents that lay that out.

Senator JOHNSON. How do we know that Hezbollah—because they've been so cooperative with the Assad regime—doesn't already have access to chemical weapons? Do we have any feel for that at all?

Secretary KERRY. I think we need to talk about that in our classified session. But let me just say to you that in terms of the opposition numbers, you see ranges up to 80-90,000, 100,000 in total opposition. You see ranges from—well, I don't want to go into all the numbers, but in the tens of thousands in terms of operative, active combatants. I've seen some recent data on the numbers of the extremists now this or there actually lower than former expectations.

I would also say to you, Syria historically has been secular. And the vast majority of Syrians, I believe, want to remain secular. It's our judgment that, and the judgment of our good friends who actually know a lot of this in many ways better than we do because it's their region, their neighborhood. I'm talking about the Saudis, the Emiratis, the Qataris, the Turks, and the Jordanians. They all believe that if you could have a fairly rapid transition, the secular component of Syria will reemerge and you will isolate—

Senator JOHNSON. Very good. That tends to argue for a more robust response.

Final question: You said this is the world's red line; I agree. So in the intervening time period before we potentially act here, how many additional countries will be supportive of this action? What support do we have right now, and what is your goal?

Secretary KERRY. Well, our goal is to have as broad a coalition and support of what we might do as is possible. We're on working that right now. But the military and the President are going to have to decide how many they actually want to have take part in the action. As I said, we already have more partners ready to do something kinetic than the military feels, under this particular operation, we need to effect that.

Now, obviously, we want them to participate because we want it to be a broad coalition. But the final numbers will have to be decided by the President and by the specific operation that he defines, together with you in the authorization.

Senator JOHNSON. I look forward to tomorrow's briefing; thanks.

Secretary KERRY. Thank you, Senator.

The CHAIRMAN. Senator Coons.

Senator COONS. Thank you, Chairman Menendez. I'd like to thank Secretaries Kerry and Hagel and Chairman Dempsey for your service to our nation and for your testimony in front of us today. I think the authorization of the use of force, I think the commitment of Americans' military strength is one of the most important issues that we will ever debate in this Congress, and I'm grateful for the opportunity to have this conversation today.

As Secretary Kerry said in his opening testimony, not just what we decide, but how we decide it will send a very important message around the world that this Congress can still function in a nonpartisan way in the interest of the people of the United States.

As I've listened to Delawareans in recent days, I think they reflect a nation that is weary of war and that is weary of inadvertently repeating some of the challenges of our engagement in Iraq. I have heard specific and pointed concerns that we not rush into action based on uneven or inaccurate intelligence, that we not be drawn into a civil war we don't fully understand or where we can't quite discern the good guys from the bad guys, and, more than anything, that we not commit to an open-ended participation, a direct military invasion and an occupation of a country and a part of the world that is often confounding and is full of competing priorities.

Having reviewed the intelligence this morning in a classified briefing, having participated in a number of briefings from you and folks leading in your agencies and departments, I am persuaded that this is not that circumstance, that the intelligence is solid, that we have in this instance a clear violation of a longstanding global red line against the use of chemical weapons, as you've stated, something embedded in America's statutes and in our treaty commitments, something that is a truly global standard.

My view, as I've watched both the images on TV that were presented at the beginning of this hearing, and as I've spoken to family and friends and neighbors at home, is that we face a real risk here if we do not act, that this is an instance where one of the world's worst dictators has steadily ratcheted up an ascending crescendo of death in his own nation.

He began with thugs, police, and the military taking on peaceful demonstrators; graduated to snipers killing innocent civilians; has used helicopters and jet fighters against his own people; has deployed cluster bombs and Scud missiles. I think over the last 2 years, there is no doubt that Bashar al-Assad and his regime is willing to go to any lengths to stay in power.

So the challenge now, for those of us who seek an appropriate path forward, is to make sure that we craft an authorization for the use of military force that responds to Americans' legitimate concerns, but still allows the administration to act in a decisive and timely way to both deter and punish the Assad regime for what they've done.

So I have a few questions for you, if I might, first to General Dempsey. And I know we've spoken to this before, but I think it is worth repeating.

How do we strike the right balance between military action that is too insignificant to actually effectively deter or degrade Assad's capabilities and one that is so decisive and overwhelming that it reaches beyond the scope of an authorization and becomes actually a regime-change effort?

General DEMPSEY. Well, Senator, I'll assure you I won't recommend an option or a set of targets that won't effectively deter and degrade. That's the task I've been given. And that now we'll continue to refine that, not just based on intelligence, but based on the resolution that comes out of this committee.

Senator COONS. And could you, in your view, accomplish that mission with an authorization that is limited in scope in terms of duration and scope, as has been discussed with Secretary Kerry, in terms of not introducing U.S. troops on the ground?

General DEMPSEY. Well, it won't surprise you to know that, as the military leader responsible for this, the broader the resolution, the less limiting, the better off I will be in crafting a set of options. But I completely defer to the Secretary of State to give me what I need to do that.

Senator COONS. Well, if I might, then, to Secretary Kerry, because our goal here is to not pass or even consider an authorization that is so narrow that it prevents any effective message to be sent here, as you said, I think in a compelling way, in your opening statement.

Our actions here are not just meant to deter Assad, but to send a strong message to Pyongyang, to Tehran, to non-state actors around the world who might use chemical weapons or might seek nuclear weapons. How do we craft an authorization? How do we take actions that are effective here in deterring other countries that are watching our decisiveness and our action in this instance?

Secretary KERRY. Well, I think the language that the administration submitted with respect to the military action necessary to degrade and deter and prevent the use of chemical weapons, specifically, is very targeted.

But, as I've said several times now, and will repeat again, I know the administration has zero intention of putting troops on the ground. And within the confines of this authorization I'm confident we'd have zero problems including some kind of prohibition if that makes you comfortable.

I would not urge an excessively pinpointed, congressionally mandated, set of targets. And I think in the course of the classified briefings, the intelligence community and the military community will make it very clear to you why that's not advisable. The general needs some latitude here to be able to make sure he can accomplish his task.

But I think the broad confines and constraints of this particular operation are not hard for us to arrive at in agreement. I'm confident we'll do it very quickly.

Senator COONS. Thank you. One of my other concerns, Mr. Secretary, is the flood of refugees and their impact on the region. In a visit in January to a Syrian refugee camp in Jordan, I was moved both by the humanitarian situation they're facing and by the very real impact that this is having on our regional allies, on Jordan, on Turkey, the destabilizing impact on Lebanon, and of course, the real impact it's potentially going to have on our close ally, Israel.

I was encouraged to hear there was a successful missile defense system test earlier today. Secretary Hagel, what steps are we taking to ensure that our allies in this immediate area, Turkey and Jordan and Israel, are able to defend themselves from a potential response by the Assad regime?

Secretary HAGEL. Well, Senator, first, Jordan, you know we have Patriot missile defense batteries in Jordan. And we also are working very closely with the Israelis. You know they have a very sophisticated Iron Dome and aerial system, missile defense system. We are in constant coordination with all the allies in the region. And as you may know, General Dempsey was just in Jordan for a commanders' meeting, which included all the senior military from the neighboring countries and our partners. So, we are closely connected with and assisting our allies on this and other issues.

Senator COONS. Thank you. Last question, Secretary Kerry, if I might. I am interested in our having a follow-on conversation about how this specific strike and this specific authorization that you're seeking can also lead to a broader strategy, a strategy for support engagement with the opposition that will lead to the diplomatic resolution of the Syrian civil war that you've spoken about repeatedly.

I don't think these are mutually exclusive. I do think it's possible for us to take action that reinforces a global red line against chemical weapons use, but to still continue to strengthen and broaden our engagement with the opposition in a way that moves toward a post-Assad Syria that is sustainable and secure. And I'd look forward to your input with us in our next hearing on that topic.

Secretary KERRY. Absolutely, Senator. I look forward to it, too. What I'd like to do is get the whole committee, maybe, to come down to the department and we could, you know, have this discussion in that confine as a committee also. And I think that might be helpful, in addition to what we do in the classified briefing tomorrow.

Senator COONS. Thank you.

Secretary KERRY. Mr. Chairman, if that—if you want to do that, I'm happy to do that follow-up.

The CHAIRMAN. Senator Flake.

Senator FLAKE. Thank you, Mr. Chairman, and thank you all for your testimony. And I want to thank you, particularly the State Department, for making information available with regard to unclassifying certain information. And also for the classified hearings that have taken place with regard to the chemical attack. I think that one would have to suspend disbelief, as you mentioned, to assume that the regime was not in charge of this.

Secretary Kerry, in your initial testimony, you asked us to ask ourselves what Assad's calculation would be if we failed to act. I think that's an appropriate question. But I think it is appropriate for us to ask you, or the administration, what is the calculation of Assad right now, when rather than after we have proof that he did engage and what he engaged in, that we're waiting for congressional authorization?

I think one would have to suspend disbelief to assume that we wouldn't be better off attacking those targets right now, or a week ago, than waiting three weeks for Congress to take action. And just drawing some parallel to the conflict in Libya, I think the President's statement was, before we went ahead and engaged in combat there, or at least along with NATO, the President said, ''I refuse to wait for the images of slaughter and mass graves to take action'' and did so without congressional authorization under the War Powers Resolution. And we had some dispute when he came back. But initially, we went ahead.

Here, we have evidence that chemical weapons were used. And how can we assure or tell our constituents that this isn't political, when we come, when you come, when the administration comes to the Congress to ask for authorization to take action that the President clearly has said he has authority to take?

Secretary KERRY. Well, Senator Flake, it's somewhat surprising to me that a member of Congress, particularly one of the Foreign Relations Committee, is going to question the President fulfilling the vision of the founding fathers when they wrote the Constitution and divided power in foreign policy to have the President come here and honor the original intent of the founding fathers in ways that do not do anything to detract from the mission itself.

Now, General Dempsey will tell you that he advised the President of the United States that not only was there not a deterioration in this mission by waiting; there might even be some advantages. And so, in fact, we're not losing anything by waiting. And I personally believe there are advantages, because we have time to work with our friends in the international community, because we have time to make the case to the American people and share with them the evidence that we have shared with you in the last days, because we have an opportunity to be able to build greater support.

And as the general has said, we can adjust to any changes or shifts that they make in that time. This does not in any way deteriorate the fundamental mission of degrading and deterring the use of chemical weapons.

Now, if at any moment Assad were foolish enough to believe that this period of waiting is somehow an invitation to do more of his criminal activity, I can assure you that the President of the United States, and I think you all, would probably speed up your process and/or the President would respond immediately.

This is working. There are defections taking place. There's great uncertainty in Syria. We are building support, a greater understanding. And I would far rather be playing our hand than his at this point in time.

So I don't think we're losing anything. I think the President made a courageous decision to take the time to build the strength that makes America stronger by acting in unity with the United States Congress.

Senator FLAKE. Well, if I may, I can certainly understand if that is a secondary goal or the primary goal that will, in this intervening time, it causes our allies to get with us. It causes Russia to put the pressure on maybe the Assad regime to get back to the table, peace talks, something like that, that's great. But purely in terms of military strategy, and I don't have a military background, but I would have to suspend disbelief, and I think all of us would, to assume that we're better off in a couple of weeks doing what we're planning to do, what we will authorize the administration to do.

General Dempsey, is there evidence that the Assad regime is right now moving some of the targets that can be moved or surrounding targets with civilians or others to make it more difficult to give effect to our strategy?

General DEMPSEY. Yeah, thanks, Senator. First, I do want to— for interest of clarity here, what I actually said to the President is the following: ''The military resources we have in place can remain in place. And when you ask us to strike, we will make those strikes effective.''

In other sessions in the principals' committee, not with the President—the President, we talked about some targets becoming more accessible than they were before. But to your question, there are, in fact, there is evidence, of course, that the regime is reacting not only to the delay, but also they were reacting before that to the very unfortunate leak of military planning. So this is a very dynamic situation.

Senator FLAKE. Secretary Hagel, you seem eager to jump in.

Secretary HAGEL. I was just going to add something that you added, Senator: And that is the international community. In addition to what the President has already noted, a nation is always stronger when it is together, when the President gets the Congress and the American people with him at the beginning; but also, we're stronger when many of the members of the international community are with us on this, I think the President feels pretty strongly that would be also an important part of whatever decision he might make.

And it doesn't end with whatever military option the President decides to go with, as we have all heard. That's all the more important; we would want the international community with us.

Senator FLAKE. Secretary Kerry, what will happen if the Congress says no and does not authorize this strike or this use of force? What will the President do?

Secretary KERRY. Well, I can't tell you what the President's going to do because he hasn't told me. But the President, as you know, retains the authority, always has the authority, had the authority to strike before coming to Congress. And that doesn't change.

But I'll tell you what will happen, where it matters. In Pyongyang, in Tehran, in Damascus, folks will stand up and celebrate. And in a lot of other capitals in parts of the world, people will scratch their heads and sign a condolence for the loss of America's willingness to stand up and make itself felt where it makes a difference to the world.

I think it would be an enormous setback to America's capacity and to our vision in the world, and certainly to the role of leadership that we play.

The CHAIRMAN. Thank you.

Senator FLAKE. Thank you, Mr. Chairman.

The CHAIRMAN. Senator Durbin.

Senator DURBIN. Thank you, Mr. Chairman. On Saturday, I was standing with a group of friends, watching the television screen with the announcement that any minute the President would make a statement. And I turned to them and said, ''I'll bet the missiles were launched and shot off hours ago, and we'll hear about it now.''

And to my surprise, of course, the President came forward and said, ''I have that authority. I've made that decision. But I'm going to respect our constitutional democracy and give the Congress—the American people through Congress—a voice in this decision.''

From where I was standing, that was good news, because for as long as I've been in Congress, House and Senate, I've argued about that congressional responsibility. Some presidents have respected it; some have not. Most of the time, Congress, in writing or in speeches, insists on being respected and being given this authority and then starts shaking when it's given, because it calls on us to be part of historic life-and-death decisions.

It's one of the toughest calls we'll ever make as members of Congress, but I salute the President for respecting the Constitution and giving us that responsibility. And I think the turnout today, on short notice in the midst of a break, on this committee, Mr. Chairman, and Ranking Member Corker, is an indication we're taking this seriously and solemnly.

I'll also note to Senator Kerry and also to Secretary Kerry and Secretary Hagel, we all served together some 12 years ago and faced similar awesome, historic decisions related to Iraq and Afghanistan. We saw those differently in some respects. But I voted against the Iraqi resolution and going to war in that country, and felt that the events that transpired afterwards gave me some justification for my vote.

But I voted for the war in Afghanistan, believing that it was a clear response to 9/11. We were going after those responsible for killing 3,000 innocent Americans. And we were going to make them pay a price. I still believe that was the right thing to do.

But I didn't know at the time that I voted for that authorization for use of military force I was voting for the longest war in the history of the United States and an authority to several presidents to do things that no one ever could have envisioned at that moment in history.

So, Secretary Kerry and Secretary Hagel, I take this very seriously. I understand this President. I understand his values. But I take it very seriously that the language be as precise as possible when it comes to this whole question of expanding this mission into something much larger, something that would engage us in a new level of warfare or a new authority for this President or a future president.

So I hope that we can have your word and assurance that we can work together in a bipartisan fashion to craft this in a way that it carefully achieves our goal, but does not expand authority anywhere beyond what is necessary.

Secretary KERRY. Senator, thank you. Very important statement, and you not only have my word that it will not do that, but we will work with you very, very closely, with the White House, in shaping this resolution. There's no hidden agenda. There's no subterfuge. There's no surrogate strategy here. There's one objective, and that objective is to make sure we live up to our obligations of upholding the norm with respect to international behavior on the use of chemical weapons, and that is what the President is seeking in this authorization.

Senator DURBIN. Let me speak to the issue of chemical weapons. I don't know if General Dempsey or Secretary Hagel or perhaps Secretary Kerry is the appropriate person, but the French have done an assessment of what they believe the Syrians have in terms of their chemical weapons arsenal.

General Dempsey, are you familiar with it?

General DEMPSEY. I'm not familiar with the French assessment. I'm familiar with our own.

Senator DURBIN. Well, let me ask. We have it here, a copy of it here. And it's been published. And we have talked a lot about sarin gas and other nerve agents. And what we hear from this report, and I'd ask you if it's close to what your assessment is, the Syrians have more than 1,000 tons of chemical agents and precursor chemicals, several hundred tons of sarin, representing the bulk of their arsenal.

It's also been speculated that they have the missile capability of delivering these chemical weapons in Israel, portions of Turkey, Jordan, Iraq, and beyond.

What is your assessment of their potential when it comes to the delivery and the capacity, when it comes to the amount, of chemical agents they have available?

General DEMPSEY. Our assessment very closely matches the French assessment.

Senator DURBIN. I guess my question to you, Mr. Secretary, Secretary Kerry, is, in light of the vulnerability of these countries, what has been the response of the Arab and Muslim world to this? I mean, you've listed four or five who have stepped forward to say they support our efforts. It would seem that if this danger in the region is so profound, that we would have even greater support.

Secretary KERRY. Senator, I think this is something I'd be happier discussing in greater detail with you in the closed session. There are obviously some countries for which public statements are more complicated than others. And I think we should talk about that at the other session.

Senator DURBIN. Fair enough.

General Dempsey, we saw these photographs earlier, these heartbreaking photographs. Page 3 of the Washington Post this morning, an ad by a group supporting the President's effort, has a photograph that's riveted in my mind, as a father and grandfather, of the children on the floor in shrouds, victims of this chemical agent gas attack.

What the administration is asking us for is military authority to launch additional attacks. What have you been charged with in terms of the issue of collateral damage from those attacks as it would affect innocent people and civilians in the nation of Syria?

General DEMPSEY. Senator, the guidance that we've received on targeting is to maintain a collateral damage estimate of low. And I'd just briefly, on how we come up with our assessments of collateral damage, it's based on how much we know about a target through intelligence, its proximity to civilian structures, and weapons effects as we decide what weapon to weaponeer against it.

And a collateral damage estimate of low means just that, that we will keep collateral damage lower than a certain number, which I would rather share with you in a classified setting.

That doesn't mean, by the way, that we would have the same constraint, if you will, in what damage could be done to regime personnel. So that's a separate issue, although even in that case I could probably tell you some more things in the classified setting.

Senator DURBIN. I look forward to that.

Thank you very much, Mr. Chairman.

The CHAIRMAN. Thank you, Senator.

Senator McCain.

Senator MCCAIN. Thank you, Mr. Chairman. I thank the witnesses. And may I say, John, it's very good to see Teresa here with you in good health and good spirits. And thank you. So, Teresa, I apologize for what I'm about to do to John.

Secretary KERRY. Man, there's a setup.

Senator MCCAIN. John, when you tell the enemy you're going to attack them—I'm not going to take any time on this. You tell the enemy you're going to attack them, they are obviously going to disperse and try to make it harder. I'm looking right here at an AP story report. Syria is said to be hiding weapons and moving troops. There's even open-source reporting that they may be moving some of their assets into the Russian naval base.

But let's not get—I mean, it's ridiculous to think that it's not wise from a pure military standpoint not to warn the enemy that you're going to attack.

Secretary Hagel, in the Wall Street Journal today, we read the following: ''Pentagon planners were instructed not to offer strike options that could help drive Mr. Assad from power: 'The big concern is the wrong groups in the opposition would be able to take advantage of it,' a senior military officer said.''

Is there any truth to that, Secretary Hagel?

Secretary HAGEL. Senator, as I've said, the President asked us for a range of options, and we provided him a range of options.

Senator MCCAIN. I am asking if there is any truth to the Wall Street Journal article.

Secretary HAGEL. Our options were not limited to any—

Senator MCCAIN. I would just ask if there is any truth to the story that is in the Wall Street Journal article.

Secretary HAGEL. No.

Senator MCCAIN. Thank you. Secretary Kerry, in the same Wall Street Journal article, ''The delay in providing arms to the opposition in part reflects a broader U.S. approach rarely discussed publicly, but that underpins its decision making. According to former and current U.S. officials, the current administration does not want to tip the balance in favor of the opposition for fear the outcome may be even worse for U.S. interests than the current stalemate.'' Is that story accurate?

Secretary KERRY. No.

Senator MCCAIN. Thank you.

Secretary KERRY. And by the way, can I add something, Senator? On the warning issue, I do not disagree with you about warning. In fact, the general would not disagree with you either. And we are all—

Senator MCCAIN. But the general said it would be just as easy—

Secretary KERRY. No, no. We are deeply—

Senator MCCAIN. Let us not get into that one.

Secretary KERRY. John, all I want to say to you is that there were leaks, which are the bane of everybody's existence. And the fact is that the newspapers began to carry stories about a strike and targeting well before any decisions were made. And that began a process of moving.

So now, there is at least—

Senator MCCAIN. Okay, I got it. I really would like to move onto some more important questions if you do not mind.

Secretary KERRY. Well, I thought all your questions were important, John.

[Laughter.]

Senator McCAIN. Thank you, John. That is good. I will try to re-member that.

The President said today that the purpose of the military action in Syria is not just to respond to Assad's use of chemical weapons, but to degrade his military capabilities as part of a broader strat-egy to change the momentum on the ground, and, as the President said, "allow Syria ultimately to free itself." Do you agree with that assessment, John?

Secretary KERRY. I said up front—I have said several times here, there will automatically, as a result of degrading his ability for chemical weapons, there will be downstream impact which will have an impact on his military capacity.

Senator McCAIN. And to allow—

Secretary KERRY. So I agree with the President.

Senator McCAIN. Thank you. General Dempsey, do you agree with that statement of the President?

General DEMPSEY. I agree. I have never been told to change the momentum. I have been told to degrade capability.

Senator McCAIN. Do you think, General, that without a change in momentum that Syria ultimately could free itself, Secretary Hagel?

Secretary HAGEL. Well, Senator, I think they all are connected. Degrading military capability, as you know, is a pretty significant part of momentum shifts.

Senator McCAIN. Secretary Kerry—John—over the weekend, the Wall Street Journal ran an important op-ed by Dr. Elizabeth O'Bagy—I hope you saw it—a Syria analyst at the Institute for the Study of War, who has spent a great deal of time inside Syria, in-cluding just this month. And I want to read her assessment of the situation on the ground, and I quote the story:

"The conventional wisdom holds that the extremist elements are completely mixed in with the more moderate rebel groups. This is not the case. Moderates and extremists wield control over a distinct territory. Contrary to many media accounts, the war in Syria is not being waged entirely or even predominantly by dangerous Islamists and Al-Qaeda diehards. The Jihadists pouring into Syria from countries like Iraq and Lebanon are not flocking to the front lines. Instead they are concentrating their efforts on consolidating control in the northern rebel-held areas of the country.

"Moderate opposition forces, a collection of groups known as the Free Syrian Army, continue to lead the fight against the Syrian re-gime. While traveling with some of these Free Syrian Army battal-ions, I have watched them defend Alawi and Christian villages from government forces and extremist groups. They have dem-onstrated a willingness to submit to civilian authority, working closely with local administrative councils, and they have struggled to ensure that their fight against Assad will pave the way for a flourishing civil society."

John, do you agree with Dr. O'Bagy's assessment of the opposi-tion?

Secretary KERRY. I agree with most of that. They have changed significantly. They have improved. And I said earlier, the fun-damentals of Syria are secular, and I believe will stay that way.

Senator McCAIN. And I think it is very important to point out again, as you just said, it is a secular state. They would reject radical Islamists, and they, in some cases, in the areas of which they have control, the people are demonstrating against them is the information I have.

So when we see these commentators say, well, we do not know which side will win, we do not know who the bad guys are, if you agree with this assessment, we certainly know who the bad guys are. Is that correct?

Secretary KERRY. I believe we do, for the most part.

Senator McCAIN. For the most part.

Secretary KERRY. There are some worse than al-Nusra, and they tend to be, most of them, in the northern area and the east.

Senator McCAIN. I thank you. And again, I would like to ask you again, can you assure the committee that the administration does not see a protracted stalemate and conflict in Syria as somehow a good thing or a goal of U.S. policy?

Secretary KERRY. The goal of U.S. policy is not a stalemate. The goal is a negotiated solution which results in the departure of Assad and the free choice of the Syrian people for their future.

Senator McCAIN. And finally, I would like to ask again, if we reject this resolution, does it not send a serious, as you already said, a seriously bad message to our friends and allies alike, encourages our enemies, and would dispirit our friends, particularly those fighting in Syria, but not only here, but around the world?

Secretary KERRY. Senator McCain, I have gotten to know my counterparts in the Mideast particularly well because of the number of crises and initiatives that we have had to deal with in that region. And I cannot emphasize enough how much they are looking us to now, making judgments about us for the long term, and how critical the choice we make here will be, not just to this question of Syria, but to the support we may or may not anticipate in the Middle East peace process, to the future of Egypt, to the transformation of the Middle East, to the stability of the region, and other interests that we have.

There is no way to separate one thing from all of the rest. Relationships are relationships, and they are integrated. And that is why this is so important.

Senator McCAIN. But I would also emphasize, if it is the wrong kind of resolution, it can do just as much damage, in my view. I thank you.

Thank you, Mr. Chairman.

The CHAIRMAN. Thank you, Senator.

Senator Udall?

Senator UDALL. Thank you. Thank you very much. And I thank all the witnesses for their testimony and for their service here today. And I also want to thank Chairman Menendez for the way he has conducted this hearing.

Like everyone here, I deplore what Bashar al-Assad has done to his own people by attacking them with chemical weapons. Assad has committed an atrocious crime so heinous that international law singles it out as an assault deserving of international action.

But let there be no mistake. I fully agree his horrific acts deserve an international response. But what should that response be? That is why we are here today, to ask that question and many others. And I hope this hearing will do more than just rubber stamp a decision that has already been made by this administration. I have grave concerns about what the administration is asking of us, of our military, and of the American people.

Here is the situation as I see it. With limited international support, we are being told the United States must retaliate for the use of chemical weapons with a surgical bombing campaign of our own. We are being told that we are bombing in order to send a message. But what message are we sending? To the international community, we are saying once again the United States will be the world's policeman. You break a law, and the United States will step in.

We are on shaky international legal foundations with this potential strike, and we need to know whether we have exhausted all diplomatic and economic sanction options to affect Syria's behavior. We need to increase our attention on the source of Assad's ability to continue to ruthlessly kill his own people, and that is support from nations, including Russia and China, who are cynically trying to hold the moral high ground. Assad would not be able to maintain his grip on power if he were not being supported from outside.

The full force of international outrage should come down on those nations that are refusing to allow the U.N. to act and find a solution.

And finally, I see this potential bombing campaign as a potential next step toward full-fledged war. We have been here before. The Iraq War began as an international effort to kick Saddam Hussein out of Kuwait, and then years of a no fly zone and air strikes to prevent Saddam from threatening his neighbors or reconstituting his arsenal of chemical weapons. And as we all know, this limited military action eventually led to what is one of the biggest blunders in U.S. foreign policy, a war that I voted against. Many who voted for it came to regret that vote.

Americans are understandably weary. After the fiasco of Iraq and over a decade of war, how can this administration make a guarantee that our military actions will be limited? How can we guarantee that one surgical strike will have any impact other than to tighten the vice grip Assad has on his power, or allow rebels allied with Al-Qaeda to gain a stronger foothold in Syria?

I take our role extremely seriously here, like many of the other Senators have said, and I will hear the President and his team out. The President made the right decision to pursue an authorization for the use of military force. I hope these hearings will give the American people the answers they deserve, but there are troubling questions that need to be answered.

And, Secretary Kerry, I want to start with you. You have assured the American people—I watched your national television performances that the U.S. action will not include, and I think you have said this here today, will not include the use of ground troops, that it will be limited in nature to deter Assad and others from using weapon of mass destruction. Yet the draft authorization of force proposed by the administration states that it would allow the President to use the armed forces, and I quote here, ''as he determines to be necessary and appropriate in connection with the use of chemical weapons or other weapons of mass destruction in the conflict with Syria.''

Now, this is a very open-ended proposal with no specific limits on types of forces that would be used, with no limit on their duration. Why was it proposed in a way that it conflicts with these statements of no ground troops? And what kind of language, Secretary Kerry, or the precise language are you willing to back in terms of showing the American people that we really mean what we say in terms of no boots on the ground?

Secretary KERRY. Senator, all good questions, and I will respond to all of them. But I want to address sort of the suspicion and concern that you have, which is appropriate. I think everybody understands that Iraq left a lot of folks reeling for some period of time, so it is appropriate to ask the questions you have asked. But please let me try to emphasize, this is not sending a message per se. This is having an effect, an impact. This is taking action to achieve something more than just a message. It is to degrade his current capacity. It will make it harder for him to do that in the future, and it will also facilitate our ability to hold him accountable in the future if he does, and he will know that. So this will affect his calculation. That is number one. That is not just a message.

Senator UDALL. Secretary Kerry, by degrading his capacity, do you not, in fact, make him weaker and make the people out there, like al-Nusra, and Al-Qaeda, and these other extremist forces, stronger? And this is what I want General Dempsey to talk about in a little bit, too.

Secretary KERRY. Well, I am happy—

Senator UDALL. Could you answer that? Could you answer that?

Secretary KERRY. I am happy—

Senator UDALL. By degrading him, you make these extremist forces stronger, do you not?

Secretary KERRY. No, I do not believe you do. As a matter of fact, I think you actually make the opposition stronger, and the opposition is getting stronger by the day now. And I think General Idris would tell you that, that he is not sitting around. His daily concern is not the opposition but Assad and what Assad is doing with his scuds, with his airplanes, with his tanks, with his artillery to the people of Syria.

But I think it is important also to look at this because you raised the question of does this not make the United States the policeman of the world. No. It makes the United States a multilateral partner in an effort that the world, 184 nations strong, has accepted the responsibility for. And if the United States, which has the greatest capacity to do that, does not help lead that effort, then shame on us. Then we are not standing up to our multilateral, and humanitarian, and strategic interests.

Now that said—

Senator UDALL. Can I stop you, Secretary Kerry, just on that one—

Secretary KERRY. Any time.

Senator UDALL [continuing]. Because if you are talking about multilateral efforts, what we are talking about is the world being able—this is a breach of a treaty. And the world put within the United Nations that enforcement mechanism, and what we have done here with Russia and China holding up the ability of the U.N. to act, we have just turned aside as a result of that—

Secretary KERRY. Well, Senator, with all due respect—

Senator UDALL. We should be standing up—we should be standing up and making sure that they are condemned, those countries that are not allowing us to move forward to find a solution where the solution should reside. So I just—

Secretary KERRY. Well, Senator, I do not disagree that we should be finding a solution where it resides. But the fact is that just a few weeks ago—just a few weeks ago—at the U.N., we sought a condemnation of a chemical attack without blame, without citing Assad, without saying who was responsible, simply a condemnation of a chemical attack. And the Russians blocked it.

Senator UDALL. Right.

Secretary KERRY. So we have no illusions. Yes, is the U.N. Security Council having difficulties at this moment performing its functions? Yes. Does that mean the United States of America and the rest of the world that thinks we ought to act should shrink from it? No. And that is really what is at test here.

I would urge you—you said how do we know it will not result in X, or Y, or Z happening if we do not do it. Let me ask you. It is not a question of what will happen if we do not do it. It is a certainty. Are you going to be comfortable if Assad, as a result of the United States not doing anything, then gases his people yet again, and the world says, why did the United States not act?

History is full of opportunity of moments where someone did not stand up and act when it made a difference. And whether you go back to World War II, or you look at a ship that was turned from the coast of Florida and everybody on it lost their lives subsequently, to German gas, those are the things that make a difference. And that is what is at stake here.

And I would say to you, you know, these are troubling questions. It is a guarantee that if the United States does not act together with other countries, we know what Assad will do. That is a guarantee. I cannot tell you what is guaranteed that some country will do if we do act, but I know what will happen if we do not. And I am pretty darn clear that a lot of things that people think will happen will not happen if the United States acts. It will, in fact, have enforced this international standard with respect to the use of chemical weapons.

And if the multilateral institution set up to do it, the Security Council, is being blocked and will not do it, that does not mean we should turn our backs and say there is nothing we can do. That is not the case. And we did it in Bosnia, and it made a difference. We saved countless numbers of lives, and I believe, the President of the United States believes, we can do that now.

Senator UDALL. Well, I do not believe that we should have given up so easily on using the United Nations—

Secretary KERRY. We have not given up—

Senator UDALL. Yes, we have. We have not taken Russia to task. We have not taken China to task. And that is what we should be pointing out at this point.

The CHAIRMAN. The time—

Senator UDALL. Well, I mean—

The CHAIRMAN. The time of the Senator has expired.

Senator UDALL. I want to respectfully disagree with you, and say also I very much appreciate your service. I know that you are trying very, very hard to find on the diplomatic side as Secretary of State, a peaceful resolution.

Thank you for your courtesy. Sorry for going over.

The CHAIRMAN. Senator Barrasso?

Senator BARRASSO. Thank you very much, Mr. Chairman. Thank you for being here.

Over Labor Day weekend in Wyoming, I heard from people all across the State. All believe what is happening is Syria is awful, despicable, do have concerns about the administration and what the plan really is, what a strategy really is. They want to know what the core national security interests of the United States are that are at stake in Syria, what our ultimate goal of proposed military strikes is, and what happens if the strikes are not effective.

And to that end, Mr. Chairman, what exactly is it that we are going to be voting on. Is it what the White House has set forward, and when are we going to see the specifics? I think Senator Durbin also asked about the narrowness or the expanse of what we will be voting—and would we be voting within the next 24 hours?

The CHAIRMAN. The chair is working with the ranking member and others to come to an agreed upon text that we believe would meet the goals of achieving the ability for the administration to pursue the military action they have sought the Congress' support for in a way that would allow them to have the maximum ability to succeed in that action, and by the same token, tailor it sufficiently so that this is not an open-ended engagement, and specifically not with boots on the ground, American troops on the ground.

We are not there yet. It is our aspiration to try to get there before the end of the day, and then to look forward to the possibility of a markup tomorrow. We will see if we can get there, and if we do, we will give all members ample notice of that time.

We start off in the morning, as I have said, with a classified briefing, and we will move from there.

Senator BARRASSO. Thank you, Mr. Chairman.

Mr. Secretary, I appreciate you coming to Congress to seek legislative authorization for the military action. President Obama specifically asserted on Saturday that he already had authority.

Now, when the British Parliament rejected a motion supporting UK participation, the prime minister specifically said that he would respect the will of the British people, and there would be no British military intervention. Where does President Obama stand with that now that he has come to Congress?

Secretary KERRY. He intends to win the passage of the resolution.

Senator BARRASSO. And on the case that he does not, is the plan that he—

Secretary KERRY. Well, we are not contemplating that—

Senator BARRASSO. Thank you.

Secretary KERRY [continuing]. Because it is too dire.

Senator BARRASSO. We talked a little bit about the risks of delays. There are already reports that by delaying military action, that Assad is moving military assets—hardware, troops—to civilian neighborhoods. Reports indicate that Russia plans to send an anti-submarine ship and missile cruiser to the Mediterranean in the next few days.

I wonder what this means to our contingency planning and what this impact is going to be for our military operations.

General DEMPSEY. There are already four Russian warships in the eastern Med, and if they are staying a respectful distance, I do not see that as a factor.

Senator BARRASSO. Has the administration created—conducted perhaps a threat assessment of how Russia, how Iran, how Hezbollah is going to respond to a U.S.-led attack? And what response do we expect from Syria's allies, including, you know, Russia, Iran, Hezbollah, to the military action?

Secretary KERRY. We all agree that that would be best handled in a classified session.

Senator BARRASSO. In terms of what success looks like, I think Senator Udall specifically, you know, said what happens if gases are used again. I am wondering if we do a limited strike as proposed and still Assad goes back and uses chemical weapons on his people. Then that engenders an entire new set of hearings, and how does this end? Where are we a month from now?

General DEMPSEY. Well, as I said, Senator, there is—we are preparing several target sets, the first of which would set the conditions for follow-on assessments, and the others would be used if necessary. And we have not gotten to that point yet.

What we do know is that we can degrade and disrupt his capabilities, and that should put us in a better position to make the kind of assessment you are talking about.

Secretary KERRY. Let me add to that if I can, John. Senator Feinstein brought this up today at the meeting at the White House. It would not be sensible to pass this resolution with a view to degrading his capacity and preventing him from doing it, if he were foolish enough to do it again. The general does have follow-on the possibilities.

And since the objective would remain the same, it would be important for Assad himself to know that you have not limited this to one specific moment with respect to chemical weapons. You can still have a limited authorization, but with respect to chemical weapons, it would be a huge mistake to deprive General Dempsey and company of their options to enforce what we are trying to achieve.

Senator BARRASSO. Trying to achieve, Mr. Secretary, the negotiated departure of Assad, you keep mentioning trying to get him to do this from the negotiating table. It seems to me that somebody who will, as Senator Coons said, go to any length to stay in power to the point of even using chemical weapons against his people, that instead would he be just driven to a more serious level of determination to keep power rather than the negotiation table?

Secretary KERRY. John, that is a very appropriate question. The answer is I do not believe so, and there are a number of reasons why I do not believe so. And most of them are best discussed, and I look forward to it with you in the private session.

But there are very strong indications from a number of discussions that have taken place between countries and individuals over the last months that Assad would not necessarily avoid making a different decision under certain circumstances. So I think we ought to leave it at that, but in the private session, I think we ought to dig into it.

Senator BARRASSO. I was going to ask about the chemical weapon stockpiles, and maybe you want to reserve this for the discussion tomorrow as well in terms of steps that we could take in terms of command and control of the regime's chemical weapons stockpiles to make sure that these things are protected in a way that could not continuously be used.

Secretary KERRY. Absolutely, and I want you to know, and this is, again, something that ought to be done in the other session. But I will just say generically, that General Dempsey and his team have taken great pains, at the instruction of the President of the United States, to make certain that whatever we do does not make it—does not make people less safe, or potentially more exposed to weapons, or that those weapons would have less control and so forth. All of these things have entered into the calculation.

Senator BARRASSO. Thank you. Thank you, Mr. Chairman.

The CHAIRMAN. Thank you, Senator Barrasso. Just one add-on to my original response to you. The resolution as sent to us by the administration will not be the resolution that we will be working on, but it is a good opening as to what the desires are and intentions are. But it will not be the specific resolution we will be working off of.

Senator Murphy.

Senator MURPHY. Thank you very much, Mr. Chairman, Secretary Kerry, Secretary Hagel, General. Thank you very much for being with us and for taking so much time with us.

We all are referencing the conversations that we have had over the last week. I have never frankly seen a greater level of public engagement on an issue since, frankly, the healthcare reform debate of 2009. And while there are certainly hardliners that have come to me with a resolution that we should go in or many more with a resolution that we should stay out, most people see both sides of this issue. And they frankly appreciate the fact that they have an American President who has taken so much time and put in so much thought into arriving at this decision, even if they disagree. And they frankly appreciate even more the fact that this President trusts them and trusts their elected representatives enough to bring this conversation to the United States Congress, albeit the fact that it may be a little messy to get from point A to point B.

And so, given all of the commotion that we will hear from our constituents, that maybe more than anything else comes out to me loud and clear.

I guess when I look at this question, I see two questions inherent in the one. One, we have to ask ourselves is there a moral or national security imperative. And I think you have very plainly made the case, as has the President, that there have been atrocities committed that we cannot let stand, and a country that has very vital security interests to the United States.

But there is a second question, and that is the one that I have trouble with and, I think, some of my colleagues have trouble with, and that is this. Will our action lesson the acuity of that moral atrocity or advance our national security interests? There both has to be a problem that needs to be solved and then a way solve it, and that is why I struggle with this.

And frankly, I do not think the fact that I and many others struggle with that question means that we lack courage or that we are, frankly, enabling the Syrian regime. I just think it is that we wonder whether there is a limit to the ability of American military power to influence the politics on the ground in the Middle East. And clearly, though there is not some direct linkage between what happened in Iraq and what happened in Syria, it does chill the ability of people to believe that America's military might can influence politics on the ground in Syria after they have watched the last 10 years.

The second problem people have is this question of escalation. And I think one of the most important things, Secretary Kerry, that you said in your prepared remarks was this: You said that we would be prepared to respond to, as you stated, a miscalculation by Assad, whether it be in reprisals against his own people or attacks against our allies in the region. That we would be prepared to be respond without going to war. Now, some people will find that statement a little incongruous. How do you respond without going to war?

And so, let me maybe ask the question this way. There are a variety of responses from Assad. He could launch another chemical weapons attack against his own people. He could launch a ferocious conventional weapons attack against his own people. He could, of course—he or his allies could launch attacks against our allies in the region.

I do not expect you necessarily to explain exactly what the response will be today, but does this resolution that we are debating today give you the ability to respond to those reprisals or in any of those situations that I just outlined, responses within Syria against his own people, or responses outside of Syria against our allies, would you have to come back to Congress for a new authorization of force?

Secretary KERRY. Well—excuse me. Sorry. As I think the President has made clear and as we have seen in many of these crises over the course certainly of my career here in the Senate, I saw presidents do both, and I supported some, and I opposed others. And on a number of occasions, presidents acted without the authorization of Congress. So there is no question but that the President would have the authority, and the right, and, conceivably, the imperative to respond without any other authorization if Assad were to attack again.

And so, I cannot—you know, I cannot speak for the President in terms of what decision he would make, but he has the authority, and that right would be available to him.

Now, if I can just say quickly with respect to, you know, it is absolutely appropriate to ask the question: Will this make a difference. It's totally appropriate think about this question of escalation. But let me say something quickly about both of those. If the Congress decides not to do this, it is a guarantee, whether it is with Assad in Syria, or nuclear weapons in Iran, or nuclear weapons in North Korea, we will have invited a for-certain confrontation, at some point in time, that will require you to make a choice that will be even worse, with the potential of even greater conflict. That I guarantee you because that is the message that will be sent.

Now, there is a distinction between this and Iraq, and I understand all the Iraq—you know. We know we lived through that here. In Iraq, intelligence purported to suggest that weapon of mass destruction existed, but we did not know if they existed. And so, we had a massive invasion in order to try to find out if they existed, and we found out they did not.

Here we have weapons of mass destruction that we not only know do exist, but they have been used, not once, not twice, not three times, but multiple times we estimate in the teens, and the opposition estimates more than that. And now, we have this most recent use of weapon of mass destruction in contravention of nearly 100 years of a prohibition against their use. So—

Senator MURPHY. Yeah, but I do not think that is the dispute. The dispute is not the correlation between intelligence.

Secretary KERRY. But the dispute is—the dispute is over what you are going to do about it.

Senator MURPHY. It is the ability of the military to be influenced—

Secretary KERRY. No, no.

Senator MURPHY [continuing]. The reality on the ground.

Secretary KERRY. Chris, the dispute is what are you prepared to do about it? That is the dispute. If you believe that by doing nothing you are going to stand up for the norm and somehow reduce the threat of the use at some future time, that is your right to believe that. But I think, and the President believes deeply, and everybody at this table believes, that flies against all common sense and all human behavior.

Senator MURPHY. Mr. Secretary, let me ask just a question about Iran because I think it is very important and a compelling narrative here. Let me just ask you this. The circumstances are very different, not to trivialize what has happened in Syria, but the stakes of Iran obtaining a nuclear weapon, which could kill millions, is different than Syria killing thousands with chemical weapons, and whether or not it lessens our moral authority to make a different decision with respect to Iran just because on Syria we decide not to act.

And second, I worry about this weariness that we have talked about within the American public, that it may ultimately make it harder—I am not saying it will, but it could make it harder for us to rally the American public with respect to a response to Iran having gone through what could be at least a slightly protracted engagement with Syria.

And so, I just—I guess I want to challenge you for a second on the automatic nature of a failure to step in in Syria with respect to compromising our ability to respond in Iran.

Secretary KERRY. Well, let me just make it very, very clear. The world decided after World War I and the horrors of gas, and the trenches, and the loss of an entire generation of young people in Europe that we were never again going to allow gas to be used in warfare. And so, if all of a sudden at this moment where in the third instance it was used by Adolf Hitler to gas millions of Jews, it was used by Saddam Hussein in order to gas Iraqis and Iranians and his own people, and now it has been used by Bashar al-Assad, three people in all of history.

And if the United States knowing it and knowing that we have drawn a line that the world has drawn with us, is unwilling to stand up and confront that, it is an absolute certainty that gas will proliferate.

We have had sarin gas in a Tokyo subway. Do you really want to have a situation where that gas may be available to these groups if it continues to deteriorate, because Assad can use this gas to continue to subjugate his population that is looking for a governance that is, you know, representative, and different, and respectful of their rights? I do not know how we could live with that.

Now, is there a difference between gas and a nuclear weapon? Well, I suppose it would depend on the scale, to be honest with you. It would depend on the scale. But the world decided that chemical, biological, and nuclear are the, you know, prohibited entities of warfare, and we as a Nation and as we as a global community have struggled to try to enforce that through the years. It is hard for me to imagine that the United States would not stand with the world against that.

Now, is it going to be effective? I am convinced that what we can do will reduce the possibilities of more use of gas and degrade Assad's capacity to use this weapon. And I think it is imperative for us, as I have said again and again, we all have to take that step. But it is significantly different from what took place in Iraq originally with respect to weapons that we did not know existed. And the two just are not similar.

The CHAIRMAN. Senator Paul.

Senator PAUL. Thank you for coming today.

It is not often that I get to compliment the President. I can probably count the number of times, maybe on one hand, but when I first heard that the President was going to come to Congress, boy, was I pleasantly surprised and I was proud that he was my President. I did not vote for him and I still am opposed to him quite a few times, but I was proud that he did this.

And I was just about to stand on my feet and clap, and give him a standing ovation, and then I heard, ''Well, but if I lose the vote, I will probably go ahead and do the bombing anyway.'' And so, it does concern me. I want to be proud of the President, but every time I am just about there, then I get worried that really he does not mean it. That he is going to sort of obey the Constitution if he wins. So I heard Secretary Kerry say, ''If we win, sure. But if we lose,'' what?

I mean, make me proud today, Secretary Kerry. Stand up for us and say you are going to obey the Constitution and if we vote you down, which is unlikely, by the way. But if we do, you would go with what the people say through their Congress, and you would not go forward with a war that your Congress votes against.

Can you give me a better answer, Secretary Kerry?

Secretary KERRY. I cannot give you a different answer than the one I gave you. I do not know what the President's decision is, but I will tell you this. It ought to make you proud because he still has the constitutional authority, and he would be in keeping with the Constitution.

Senator PAUL. Well, I disagree with you there. I do not believe he has the constitutional authority. I think Congress has this.

Madison was very explicit. When he wrote ''The Federalist Papers,'' he wrote, ''That history supposes, or the Constitution supposes what history demonstrates that the executive is the branch most likely to go to war, and therefore the Constitution vested that power in the Congress.'' It is explicit and runs throughout all of Madison's writings.

This power is a congressional power and it is not an executive power. They did not say big war or small war. They did not say boots on the ground, not boots on the ground. They said, ''declare war.'' Ask the people on the ships launching the missiles whether they are involved with war or not.

If we do not say that the Constitution applies. If we do not say explicitly that we will abide by this vote, you are making a joke of us. You are making us into theater. And so, we play constitutional theater for the President.

If this is real, you will abide by the verdict of Congress. You are probably going to win. Just go ahead and say it is real, and let us have a real debate in this country, and not a meaningless debate that, in the end, the illusion is to say, ''Oh, well. We had the authority anyway. We are going to go ahead and go to war anyway.''

A couple of items.

Secretary KERRY. Senator, I assure you, there is nothing meaningless, and there is everything real—

Senator PAUL. Only if you adhere to what we vote on.

Secretary KERRY [continuing]. —about what is happening here.

Senator PAUL. Only if our vote makes a difference. Only if our vote is binding is it meaningful.

Secretary KERRY. And I will leave to the man who was elected to be President of the United States the responsibility for telling you what his decision is if and when that moment came. But the President intends to win this vote and he is not going to make prior announcements.

Senator PAUL. We have had a lot of discussion about whether or not we are going to make the world safer with this. Somehow we are going to have less chemical weapons, but I think that is an open question, and I think it is conjecture at best.

You can say, ''Oh, well. We think Assad will be less likely to launch chemical weapons after this.'' We may be able to degrade his capacity somewhat. You have got 1,000 tons. Are we going to wipe it out? Most reports I hear say we are not even probably going to directly bomb chemical weapons because of what might happen to the surrounding population. So my guess is he still will have the ability.

Most people say Assad acted very illogically. Why would he release chemical weapons on his own people when it brought the anger and enmity of the entire world? So he is already acting irrationally or illogically. Now, we are going to deter him and he is going to act in a rational manner.

I think it is equally likely that he either does it again, or he does not do it. I do not think you can say for certain which is better.

I do not know that we can say that by attacking them, he is not going to launch another chemical attack. Will the region—

Secretary KERRY. Well—

Senator PAUL [continuing]. Will the region, I have a few of them and then I will stop.

Will the region be more stable or less stable? We all say we want stability in the Middle East, and stability in the Middle East is a national interest for our country. Will it be more stable or less stable? I frankly think there are equal arguments on both sides of that.

Will Israel be more likely to suffer an attack on them, a gas attack or otherwise, or less likely? I think there is a valid argument for saying they will be more likely to suffer an attack if we do this.

Will Russia be more likely or less likely to supply more arms and get more heavily involved in this? I think there is a valid argument that they may become more likely to be involved.

Iran, more likely or less likely to be involved with this? If Iran gets involved, more likely or less likely that Israel launches a reprisal attack on Iran? There are all kinds of unknowns that I cannot tell you absolutely the answer and neither can you, but I think there is a reasonable argument that the world may be less stable because of this, and that it may not deter any chemical weapons attack.

So what I would ask is: how are we to know? How are we to go home? I have not had one person come up to me and say they are for this war. Not one person. We get calls by the thousands. Nobody is calling in favor of this war.

I did not meet, while I was home all month, I went to 40 cities. I did not have one person come up and say that they were in favor of going to war. Do they all agree it is a horrendous thing? Yes. We all agree that chemical attacks are a horrendous thing, but people are not excited about getting involved. They also do not think it is going to work, and they are skeptical of what will occur with this.

But I would appreciate your response and try to reassure the rest of us, one, that the vote is meaningful and valid, that you would adhere to it. And also, that you are convinced that all of these different items will be better, not worse, by this attack.

Secretary KERRY. Well, Senator, I would be very happy to do that. Will Israel be more likely to suffer an attack, or will they be safer? Will they be less safe? I can make it crystal clear to you that Israel will be less safe unless the United States takes this action.

Iran and Hezbollah are two of the three biggest allies of Assad. And Iran and Hezbollah are the two single biggest enemies of Israel. So if Iran and Hezbollah are advantaged by the United States not curbing Assad's use of chemical weapons, there is a much greater likelihood that at some point down the road, Hezbollah, who has been one of the principle reasons for a change in the situation on the ground, will have access to these weapons of mass destruction. And Israel will, for certain, be less secure.

Let me just say this—

Senator PAUL. But I would also argue that it would be more likely that Hezbollah will attack because of this attack in response.

Secretary KERRY. And Israel feels quite confident of its ability to deal with Hezbollah if they were to do so. You will notice that Israel has, on several occasions in the last year, seen fit to deal with threats to its security because of what is in Syria, and not once has Assad responded to that to date.

I think there are a bunch of things we should talk about in a classified session. But let me just make it very clear to you that, you know, you ask these questions, ''Will this or that be more likely to happen or not likely to happen?''

If the United States of America does not do this, Senator, is it more or less likely that Assad does it again? Do you want to answer that question?

Senator PAUL. I do not think it is known. I do not think—

Secretary KERRY. Is it more or less likely that he does it again?

Senator PAUL [continuing]. If you have the attack. I think it is unknown whether it is more or less likely whether you have the attack.

Secretary KERRY. It is unknown? Senator, it is not unknown. If the United States of America does not hold him accountable on this with our allies and friends, it is a guarantee Assad will do it again—a guarantee—and I urge you to go to the classified briefing and learn that.

Second, let me just point out to you that with respect to this question of Americans wanting to go to war. You know, you have three people here who have been to war. You have John McCain who has been to war. There is not one of us who does not understand what going to war means, and we do not want to go to war.

We do not believe we are going to war in the classic sense of taking American troops and America to war. The President is asking for the authority to do a limited action that will degrade the capacity of a tyrant who has been using chemical weapons to kill his own people.

Senator PAUL. But I think by doing so, you announce it.

Secretary KERRY. It is a limited.

Senator Paul. You announce—

Secretary KERRY. It is limited.

Senator PAUL [continuing]. By doing so, you announce in advance that your goal is not winning.

Secretary KERRY. But that is not—

Senator PAUL. And I think the last 50 years of Secretaries of Defense would say if your goal is not to win, we should not be involved.

Secretary KERRY. If people are asked, ''Do you want to go to war in Syria?'' of course not. Everybody, one hundred percent of Americans, will say no. We say no. We do not want to go to war in Syria either. It is not what we are here to ask.

The President is not asking you to go to war. He is not asking you to declare war. He is not asking you to send one American troop to war. He is simply saying we need to take an action that can degrade the capacity of a man who has been willing to kill his own people by breaking a nearly one hundred year old prohibition, and will we stand up and be counted to say, ''We will not do that.''

That is not, I just do not consider that going to war in the classic sense of coming to Congress and asking for a declaration of war, and training troops, and sending people abroad, and putting young Americans in harm's way. That is not what the President is asking for here.

General, do you want to speak at all to that?

General DEMPSEY. No, not really, Secretary. Thank you for offering.

Senator KAINE. Great. Thank you to all of you. This has been a good discussion.

I want to echo what Senator Paul, Senator Durbin, and others have said. I very much appreciate and celebrated the President's decision to bring this matter to Congress. I also believe with others that the Constitution reserves the power to initiate military action to Congress; 535 people get a vote on that. There is only one Commander-in-Chief after the vote is taken, after we do that searching inquiry, it is the Commander-in-Chief that has to decide how to execute the decided upon mission. But I applaud the President for doing it.

I view it not only as a matter of constitutional law. I view it as reflecting a very important underlying value, and the value is this: We should not put service members into initiating battle, putting people into harm's way if they do not have a consensus behind them, the American public, the political leadership behind them. To send young men and women into war, or into a military action, where they are exercising military options with a divided political leadership class is the worst thing we can do.

And so, we need to come to a consensus and then execute on that consensus whatever it is. And it would be my hope that Congress' consensus would then be what the President would do and not otherwise.

There is a basic principle at stake. I think you stated it well. It is a principle of international law and American law: n o use of weapons of mass destruction against civilians.

I don't know of a higher principle of the relations of states, of the law of nations, of sort of international legal morality than no use of weapons of mass destruction against civilians, and that is the principle that is at stake as we wrestle with this request of the President on this committee. That is a principle that is very clear.

As you said, Secretary Kerry, it is not about if the weapons of mass destruction exist—they exist. It is not just whether they will be used. They have been used. They have been used against civilians. They have been used against civilians on a massive scale, including women and children.

And so, it is a principle that is squarely at stake. We know that Bashar al-Assad does not care about the principle. Contrary to things that you have said, we know that Vladimir Putin, until he shows otherwise, does not care about the principle.

I hope Congress still cares about the principle. It is a principle of longstanding origin. Syria signed onto it, the Geneva Convention. The Soviet Union signed onto the Geneva Convention and then again, in the 1990s era, Chemical Weapons Convention as Russia under the leadership of the previous president, President Yeltsin.

So we know that there are some who don't care, but I hope that Congress shows that we do care by our action.

A couple of questions are, first, Russia. I want to associate with something that Senator Udall said earlier. The fact that they—we have not done enough to demonstrate that Russia has essentially become a pariah nation by being pro chemical weapons.

It is hard to read their action and come up with any conclusion other than the current government of Russia is pro use of chemical weapons against civilians. We should make them wear being a pro chemical weapons nation like a rotting carcass around their neck in every instance we can. So that at some point, they will ask themselves the question, do we really want to be the nation that is pro use of chemical weapons against a civilian population?

If we make that as painful as we can every day at the U.N., even if they are going to block it, we come back with another—we should make it painful every day. So that at some point, they will ask themselves the question, why do we want to carry this water for a dictator who is using chemical weapons against his own civilians?

We haven't done enough on that score. The fact that they are going to block us shouldn't dissuade us. We should do more and more and more. I think that will ultimately contribute to a political negotiation.

I want to ask you the question about the Syrian opposition's position on chemical weapons. I was unclear about their position on chemical weapons, but I understand that the opposition may have made some commitments in compacts that have been negotiated, Mr. Secretary, that they are anti-chemical weapons, that they would commit to turn over chemical weapons to the international community either if they take control of those weapons during the course of this civil war or whether they are in the lead in a post Assad government.

Can you talk about the opposition and their commitment to get rid of the stockpile of chemical weapons that is currently being used?

Secretary KERRY. Yes, we have had some discussions about that, and I hope that when the president comes here, when President Jarba comes here that he will make that position clear to all of you.

Senator KAINE. That would be very helpful. I think that would be one of the best things the opposition could do is make that plain.

There is a little bit of a confusion. I think we can talk shorthand here in ways that might make it hard for Senators and certainly the public to follow. We are here talking about military action on the same time we are saying there will be no solution to the civil war that is not a negotiated political solution. So those can seem to be at odds.

I want to state my understanding of how they fit together, and you tell me if I am right or wrong. If we take action, action to degrade the ability of Syria to use chemical weapons, action to degrade their ability to violate international law, it will take away a significant asset that they have in their battle against the opposition.

It will level the playing field by removing the ability to use chemical weapons, and it will, therefore, increase the odds that the parties will then come to the table to try to figure out that political solution. Is that the connection between the military option you are proposing and the stated end goal of a solution to the civil war only being—only being achieved through a political end?

Secretary KERRY. It is the collateral connection to it. It is not the purpose of it, but it is a collateral connection.

Senator KAINE. I don't have any other questions, Mr. Chair. I will save them for tomorrow.

The CHAIRMAN. Thank you.

Senator Markey?

Senator MARKEY. Thank you, Mr. Chairman, very much.

Without question, there is great horror and disgust at Assad's use of chemical weapons and great sympathy for the people of Syria, that their leader would use chemical weapons upon his own people and that his murderous regime is so dedicated to retaining power that they would use those weapons.

At the same time in our own country, there is great concern that we could be invoking the law of unintended consequences as we talk about using our own military in Syria. Back in 2001 and 2002, the threat obviously was that the next attack at the United States could come in the form of a mushroom cloud from Iraq. And although there were inspectors on the ground for 100 days in Iraq who could not find it before the war started, nonetheless, that war began.

And I think people are understandably apprehensive about what we are talking about right now because of what did precipitate that war in Iraq. So I continue to look forward to additional evidence being presented, and my hope is that we can act in a way that does not bog us down into the middle of a Syrian civil war.

I think there are many people who want us in the middle of the Syrian civil war, many people. But I don't think that the American people do. I think they are very wary of having our country, once again, drawn into a civil war in another country.

The concern that I think many people have is that we don't fully understand as well what the reaction of the Russians will be to this action. So, General, you—and I thank you, General and Secretary Kerry and Secretary Hagel, for your—this is a tough job, and we really appreciate the sensitivity and the professionalism with which you are handling this.

You talked about the Russians now having four vessels in Eastern Mediterranean, but you did not seem to be that concerned about it. Syria is a proxy state of Russia. They provide the military assistance, the training to Syria.

Are you concerned in any way that a strike by the United States could increase the amount of military assistance that Russia sends into the Syrian regime?

General DEMPSEY. It could, Senator. I mean, they—there is some indication that they have assured the regime that if we destroy something, they can replace it. But, you know, that is not a reason for me to hesitate to act.

And to your point, there are always unintended consequences of conflict. But as the Secretary has mentioned, we know what the consequences could be, probably would be, if we do not act.

Senator MARKEY. Thank you.

Mr. Secretary—and Teresa, you look great. You look absolutely fantastic here today.

It is my understanding that the U.N. chemical inspection team left Syria on Saturday and that U.N. Secretary Ban Ki-moon has directed the team to expedite the mission's analysis of the samples and information it has obtained. When do we expect to obtain that data and the analysis made by the U.N., and when do we expect that information to be made public?

Secretary KERRY. I am sorry. Which information?

Senator MARKEY. The United Nations inspection team.

Secretary KERRY. Senator—by the way, Mr. Chairman, I am looking over here at my successor in the United States Senate, and I don't know if there is a new initiation process here on the committee, but I notice he doesn't even get a nameplate.

[Laughter.]

Secretary KERRY. Oh, all right. I was worried about you.

Senator MARKEY. In the House, they put it up for you. So I am learning what the protocol is over here.

The CHAIRMAN. We are dealing with sequester. So you have to do it yourself.

Secretary KERRY. I thought Massachusetts was on an uneven keel here for a minute.

Senator, first of all, welcome to the committee and welcome to the Senate.

Senator MARKEY. Thank you.

Secretary KERRY. It is good to see you here.

With respect to the U.N. process, we are hearing somewhere, you know, 3 weeks, anywhere from 2 to 4 weeks, I suppose, is the range. But I think about 3 weeks is what we have been told.

Senator MARKEY. So would it be wise for us to wait for that information from the United Nations in order to ensure that there is a signal sent to the international community as to the veracity of the analysis by the United States that chemical weapons have been used?

Secretary KERRY. Well, let me speak to that because it is a very important and legitimate question. First of all, the mandate of the United Nations inspection team, which we have great respect for and we are grateful to them and to Secretary-General Ban Ki-moon for their courageous effort to go in under difficult circumstance. And we have obviously pushed for inspections in other circumstances.

The distinction here is that their mandate will only allow them to say that a chemical weapons attack took place. They have no mandate to assign blame, who did it. And Secretary-General Ban Ki-moon has reaffirmed that this is, in fact, what they won't do. They won't assign blame. They will confirm what happened.

Now can they provide additional information in terms of details and some additional evidence? The answer is yes. But will they tell us anything that we do not know today beyond a reasonable doubt? The answer is no.

They can't tell us because they don't have the technical means or the intelligence operation or the capacity to put together what we have released to the world in an unclassified document. And when you add what we have in classified form that I obviously can't go into here, we have an even more persuasive case about what has happened here.

Now let me add to that, if I can, just one more thing. Iran and Syria itself have both admitted that a chemical weapons attack took place. So Iran and Syria are already telling us an attack took place, but they've chosen the improbable and illogical notion that the opposition did it, not the regime.

Senator MARKEY. My only suggestion would be that the United States declassify a higher percentage of the information that we have so that the American people and the international community can see it. And I think that would be helpful in this whole discussion, that if we declassified, I think it would actually give more assurance to the international community.

Secretary KERRY. Senator, I understand. And I have to tell you, the unprecedented level of declassification already, according to the intel community, could possibly put at risk some sources and methods. Now one of the reasons that it was chosen to release one is somehow it leaked from someplace in the world, and it was already in several newspapers.

So, as a result of that, it was—it was further declassified. But that itself is an intercept, an actual conversation now out in public that shows the regime acknowledging its own culpability and expressing fear about the U.N. discovering it. So there is already, it seems to me, a sufficient level without tempting fate on sources and methods.

Senator MARKEY. Thank you. Thank you, Mr. Secretary.

And Secretary Hagel, if I may just quickly, on the administration's draft resolution, would that draft authorization allow the U.S. military to conduct military operations outside of Syria?

Secretary HAGEL. No.

Senator MARKEY. It would not. And would it allow military operations against foreign governments other than Syria?

Secretary HAGEL. No.

Senator MARKEY. And would it authorize military operations against nonstate actors?

Secretary HAGEL. No.

Senator MARKEY. Okay. Thank you.

Thank you, Mr. Chairman.

The CHAIRMAN. Thank you, Senator Markey.

Let me, on behalf of the committee, thank all of our distinguished witnesses. They have been testifying for in excess of 3 1/2 hours, and I appreciate their information they have imparted with the committee.

Let me say that I appreciate the thoughtfulness with which each member has come to this issue at this hearing and expressed their concerns and their views, and I have listened closely and understand some of those concerns. I have listened to my colleagues particularly express concern as to whether the actions we conceive would, in fact, deter or degrade the ability of Assad to pursue chemical weapons attacks in the future, and I am reminded in a much different context of an experience I had in my own life.

General Dempsey is actually originally from my area, Jersey City and Bayonne. And I grew up in a tough neighborhood, and we had a bully in the neighborhood. And I was walking along the street one day, and he just slapped me in the face. And I went away and told my mom, and she said avoid him. Avoid him, just avoid him.

And a week later, I saw the bully again, and I did all my best to avoid him, and this time he punched me in the nose, and it was bloody. And I went back to her and said, you know, mom, I tried to avoid him. She said, well, just avoid him.

And it wasn't until the third time when we were by a construction site that I got a piece of wood and whacked the bully, and that was the end of it. I never got whacked again.

It is not quite this, but there is a lesson to be learned. Assad has made a calculation now, by inching up several times, that he can use chemical weapons; or he believes he can use chemical weapons without consequence. And in doing so, there is a global message that, in fact, other state actors and other nonstate actors may believe they can do so as well.

That is a critical challenge for the national security of the United States, and I hope members will consider that as we move toward final action.

I want to advise members, I think we are close to a text on a resolution and so that they should consider that it is likely that we may very well be in a business meeting sometime after the classified hearing tomorrow morning, and we look forward to working with all of the members of the committee.

Senator Corker, is there anything else?

Senator CORKER. I think you have said it well enough. I want to thank the witnesses for spending this much time not only in the hearing, but also in advance of the hearing.

I look forward to the classified meeting tomorrow, and I want to thank all the members for incredible thoughtfulness throughout all of this. And I appreciate everybody coming back to be a part of this and taking it so seriously, which I think everybody will do.

Thank you.

The CHAIRMAN. With the thanks of the committee, this hearing is adjourned.

[Whereupon, at 6:10 p.m., the hearing was adjourned.]

ADDITIONAL MATERIAL SUBMITTED FOR THE RECORD

RESPONSES TO QUESTIONS FOR THE RECORD SUBMITTED TO SECRETARY OF
STATE JOHN KERRY FROM SENATOR JOHN BARRASSO

Question. Is the United States required by law to use force against the government of Syria for their use of chemical weapons against their own people? Please provide the specific law which mandates that the United States take military action.

Answer. No.

Question. What is the administration's overall strategy in Syria?

Answer. We are committed to ending the violence in Syria and helping it become a stable country that will support our national security interests in the heart of the Middle East, including by controlling, and eventually dismantling, its chemical weapons stocks as well as containing and eventually removing terrorist groups from its soil.

Our goal is a peaceful political transition that results in Assad's departure and the establishment of a representative and legitimate government that represents the will of all Syrians.

The formula for this peaceful political transition already exists—it is laid out in the Geneva Communiqué—and Russia, the UN, EU, Arab League, and other key countries support it.

The Communiqué calls for a transitional government chosen by the mutual consent of the Assad regime as well as the opposition. That means that both sides will have to choose people who will protect not one side or the other, but the rights of all Syrians.

The opposition supports this goal; the Assad regime does not.

To persuade Assad to engage in serious negotiations, the United States and key partners are increasing the scope and scale of assistance to the moderate opposition, the Syrian Coalition and the Supreme Military Council, while working to stymie the growing influence of extremists.

Question. How do the military strikes play into the administration's overall policy on Syria and the region?

Answer. Our objective is to deter further chemical weapons use by the regime, to degrade their capacity to carry out future chemical weapons attacks, and to enforce the international norm against chemical weapons use so that regimes like Syria, Iran and North Korea don't believe that they can act with impunity.

The indiscriminate and large-scale use of chemical weapons by the regime on August 21 violates clearly established international norms against the use of chemical weapons and the law of war. The international community has been engaged in a sustained effort to eliminate the use of chemical weapons, including in response to the agonizing suffering caused by those weapons during World War I. So it should not be surprising that leaders from around the world, including the United Nations Secretary General, the Arab League, and NATO, have condemned the brutal August 21 attacks as violating these international norms.

Countries like Turkey, Jordan and Israel feel threatened by the Syrian regime's growing use of chemical weapons. The egregious Syrian behavior threatens to further destabilize this important region, and thereby threaten core U.S. security interests.

The President stated that he has no interest in an open-ended U.S. involvement in Syria. As we've long made clear—and as the events of August 21 reinforce—it is imperative that we reach a comprehensive and durable political solution to the crisis in Syria. We do not believe there is a military solution to the conflict in Syria. The United States remains fully invested in the Geneva peace process, and we will continue working with Russia and other international partners to move toward a political transition based on the framework laid out in the Geneva Communiqué. The responses that the President is considering now are specifically designed to deter and prevent further use of chemical weapons by the Assad regime and to reduce the risk of proliferation of these weapons.

RESPONSES TO QUESTIONS FOR THE RECORD SUBMITTED TO SECRETARY OF DEFENSE CHUCK HAGEL FROM SENATOR JOHN BARRASSO

Use of Chemical Weapons

Question. On August 21, 2013, the Assad regime again crossed President Obama's red line resulting in the death of 1,429 civilians in Syria. What standard did the administration use to determine that the chemical weapons use on August 21 warrants military action while the previous use of chemical weapons did not?

Answer. As I've said before, military action should be a last resort. Once we determined that chemical weapons (CW) had been previously used, the President reiterated his warning to Assad while simultaneously enhancing U.S. military support to the opposition. We hoped increased support to the opposition would signal to Assad our seriousness on this matter, and dissuade him from employing these heinous weapons again. Assad chose to ignore our warning and proceeded to use CW again, this time on a much larger scale, flaunting his disregard for international norms. It is imperative that we demonstrate to Assad that his use of CW will elicit a strong international response, one that will deter him and degrade his capabilities to employ indiscriminate weapons against his own people.

Budget

Question. When the Department of Defense submitted its budget request at the beginning of the year, it made clear that there were shortfalls in the Overseas Contingency Operations budget and even seemed to indicate there were also shortfalls in certain parts of the base operating budget.

a. What is the cost estimate for the military action being proposed by President Obama?

b. Do we have the resources available for military actions in Syria?

c. What U.S. forces and capabilities are currently available to engage targets in Syria?

d. Will a supplemental appropriation request be required?

Answer. a. The President's guidance is that the operations in Syria be limited in scope, and we expect the costs to be limited as well. Costs will depend on the details of the operation. A reasonable range of costs is tens to hundreds of millions of dollars. I cannot be more precise at this time.

b. While the fact that this operation comes toward the end of a difficult fiscal year does limit flexibility, the Department will use remaining operating funds to finance any incremental costs in FY 2013. We will have to determine how to finance any incremental FY 2014 costs after we know the status of Congressional action on our FY 2014 budget request.

c. From an unclassified perspective, the Navy has four guided missile destroyers in the eastern Mediterranean and the aircraft carrier USS Nimitz with its supporting vessels in the Red Sea. However, the specific force structure depends on final decisions.

d. The administration has indicated that it does not currently plan to submit a supplemental funding request.